SELF-HEALING POWER AND RELAXATION MEDITATION:

BEGINNERS GUIDE TO MINDFULNESS THERAPY. STOP ANXIETY, LIVE STRESS FREE AND DECLUTTER YOUR MIND. BEDTIME STORIES: FALL ASLEEP AND

AWAKENING BETTER

Peace of Soul & Brain Foundation

TABLE OF CONTENTS

Introduction

Meditation is about taming your mind. A lot of people struggle with trying to overcome anxiety, despair, agitation, and other habitual thought patterns that they may find difficult to break out of. Taming the mind through mindful meditation is how you give yourself control of your own well-being once more. Meditation will bring you a sense of fullness and completion. Believe it or not, it is the only way to truly achieve tranquility that is easily accessible to everyone on this planet. True, there may be other temporary forms of serenity, but nothing will come close to bringing you the long-term peace that you seek no matter what you may be going through in your life the way meditation will. And that is why we learn to meditate.

Meditation has been practiced traditionally for hundreds, if not thousands, of years. It is not something that just came about overnight as a new trend. Meditation is something that is inherent in all human beings, something that we all have in us to be able to do. Many are already reaping the benefits of what meditation has to offer, and now, it's time for you to start doing the same thing.

Learning to meditate is just like learning any other skill you put yourself through. When you learn to meditate, you exercise your mind muscles that you never or rarely worked on before. Meditation takes consistent practice for you to be more aware, mindful, and focused. There is no such thing as perfect meditation. Along your journey of mindful meditation, you will sometimes lose focus, your mind will wander, and you will also forget to follow your breath. Just remember that this is okay. Remember that it is a journey and not a destination.

This is why a lot of people find meditation to be a helpful practice. Those who avidly do this find that their mind is peaceful and free from worries and mental discomfort, making it easier for them to achieve happiness compared to those who do not practice meditation at all. If you have never tried it, you may scoff at the idea of how sitting quietly for a few minutes every day is going to make a difference in your life, but you would be surprised.

Think about it. What is it that successful people and motivational speakers often say they do as part of their daily routine? That's right; they spend a few hours meditating in the morning. Clearly, it's working for them, isn't it? They're able to go through life, even with the struggles that may come their way, with a positive attitude, and they don't let stress get the best of them. Now, you don't necessarily have to practice meditation in the morning the way they do; you can meditate at any time that works best for you. There is no hard and fast rule. You can even meditate more than once a day if you need to, and you find that it helps. You make your own rules according to what works best for you.

By spending a few minutes each day, training your mind and making meditation part of your routine, you will discover that your mind gradually is able to find peace a lot easier, and finding happiness is something that doesn't seem so elusive anymore, even if you have certain challenges that you may be going through in your life. Even in the most difficult circumstances, you will find that you are able to remain calm, steady, and still able to look at the bright side of life.

Learning to control our minds is one of the most difficult things we can do. It's easy to let our thoughts get the best of us, which is why it is so easy to be consumed by negativity, and external circumstances can affect us to such an extent. The thing about this is, we don't even realize just how severely we are affected by it all because we are not really thinking too much about it. Fluctuations in our moods seem like a normal, everyday occurrence, and we brush it off as being part of life, and we can't control it. But that's where you would be wrong.

The reason is that you can control it with meditation. Create that inner space and clarity in your mind that will enable you to always be in firm control of your thoughts, despite the circumstances you may be facing. Meditation is how you find that mental balance, so you are never at one extreme or the other (never too sad or never so happy). It is always about finding the right balance. You have always been told you need to live a balanced life and eat balanced meals, so why not have a balanced mind, too? Meditation is a way of bringing your mental clarity and change the way you look at the world around you.

Chapter 1 Stress and Anxiety

From the outside, the distinctions between stress and anxiety can be difficult to detect. Both of these can result in sleepless nights, weariness, constant anxiety, lack of focus, and irritability. Even physical symptoms such as rapid heart rates, muscle pain, and headaches can affect people who are stressed or diagnosed with an anxiety disorder. For symptoms that may seem interchangeable, it can be hard to determine when to work on deep breathing and when to pursue medical assistance.

In short, stress is the response of your body to a stimulus and is usually a short-term experience. Stress may be either positive or negative. When stress comes into play and helps you get that deadline, it's positive. It's negative when stress leads to sleeplessness, poor concentration, and diminished ability to do things that you regularly do. Stress in any particular circumstance is a reaction to a threat.

Anxiety, on the other hand, is a chronic, stress-related mental health disorder. After the threat is mediated, anxiety doesn't fade away. Anxiety hangs over the long-distance and can cause considerable impairments in social, productivity, and other important functioning fields.

Most people experience occasional stress and anxiety. Stress is a demand imposed on your brain or body. People report being stressed when they are asked to make multiple competing demands. An event which makes you feel overwhelmed or nervous can trigger the feeling of stress. Anxiety is a sense of fear, worry, or discomfort. It can be a response to stress, or it can happen in people who cannot identify important stressors in their lives.

Anxiety and stress can help you overcome a problem or dangerous situation in the short-term. Symptoms of daily stress and anxiety include stressing about finding a job, nervousness before an extensive examination, or humiliation in certain social situations. If we have no fear, we may not be inspired to do what we need to do (e.g., preparing for this big test).

However, it can imply a more serious problem when stress and anxiety start messing with your daily life. It may be time to seek treatment if you avoid situations because of irrational fear, constant worrying, or severe anxiety about a traumatic experience weeks after it occurred.

What Do Stress and Anxiety Feel Like?

Stress and anxiety can cause physical and psychological symptoms. People encounter various stresses and anxieties. Common physical signs are:

- Dizziness

- Diarrhea

- Muscle tension

- Change in appetite

- Trouble sleeping

- Rapid breathing

- Sweating

- Headache

- Fatigue

- Shaking

- Frequent urination

- Fast heartbeat

- Stomachache

People with long periods of stress and anxiety will experience negative health outcomes. They are more likely to experience diabetes, heart disease, hypertension, and even depression and panic disease.

Eustress and Distress

Eustress translates to "good stress," a term that comes from a very significant insight amongst people. If you have a positive view of any scenario, you will never generate enough hormones to hurt you in the long run. Think of young people seeking strong sensations— such as those young people who go up in a helicopter and sprint directly from there on a ski hill without trying to think of the avalanches this could trigger.

In the field of stress science, researchers early on suggested that this situation should lead to a significant long-term stress reaction among these young people. When the researchers studied people in search of strong sensations, they found that these people created sufficient stress hormones to offer themselves a real "high," but not enough that they could hurt each other in the long-term.

Distress, on the contrary, refers to "bad stress." If you take me from a helicopter on a ski hill, I will be in total distress, even with my skis on, because I understand this entirely in an adverse way. I don't want to be there and do not want to participate in an activity that I think is too dangerous. Because I have a negative interpretation of the situation personally, I can produce sufficient stress hormones to cause long-term harm.

The scenario is similar in both situations (springing from a helicopter to a ski hill), but the person who interprets it positively will not be affected by the negative effects of stress, while the person with a negative interpretation is affected.

This example shows how the perception of a situation can significantly influence the development of good stress (eustress) or bad stress (distress).

Over the last few decades, we have devoted a lot of our focus to how stress is always negative, and we can do nothing. This is a false statement. In demonstrating that a stress response arises from an understanding of a situation as threatening (relative stress) or not, research has made it clear that we have immense power over our stress response. Nonetheless, it is important to explore how chronic stress takes root and can render us sick until we see how we can manage stress more effectively. If you know about the long, rolling road that can lead to chronic stress, I hope that the next time you come across it, you are able to avoid it.

Chapter 2 Causes of Stress

Work

Work is such a popular source of stress that an entire scientific journal is dedicated to the study of it. For the past thirty years, Work and Stress has covered the impact of work and organizations on health. The American Psychological Association found that 65 percent of Americans named work as their top source of stress. It's not hard to understand why. We all want to do well at work because how we perform determines how much money we make, how we perceive ourselves, and how others perceive us.

Work is also where we spend most of our time. A 40-hour work week is often not reality, as work demands more and more of our hours. Many people find it hard to say no at work because they believe that if they don't say yes, their jobs may be in jeopardy. We often agree to new responsibilities as we wonder how we're going to fit one more task into our ever-lengthening day.

- **Work-Life Balance**

Even if you love what you do, the demands of the modern workplace can leave you feeling stressed and looking for balance because your life feels out of whack. What does work-life balance really mean? For each person, it means something different. I am now a remote worker who, as an academic, traveled as often as possible for the past 20 years during academic breaks and to far-flung conferences during the school year. And no matter how much I love my job; I can't imagine having only two weeks off. Some people love working from home or their local café or co-working space, whereas others feel disconnected and lonely and miss the interaction that office life brings.

Finances

In a capitalist society where we constantly buy new and better items, it would seem that we're set up to be stressed about money. Money stress is often related to work stress because of salaries and benefits. In the United States, where our social welfare benefits are not very generous, it's on us to save enough to cover emergencies while still paying for our day-to-day expenses. Credit card debt is increasing as we spend more than we make and use debt to fill the gap. And with student loan debt in the trillions, too many of us will be paying back loans for a really long time. If you have children, planning for their college expenses can seem like a herculean task as tuition costs get higher and higher.

Family and Friends

The relationships you have with family and friends can be both a blessing and a curse when it comes to stress. If you have loving, supportive relationships, then family is your refuge from stress and can be a key factor in reducing the impact of stress in your life. However, if your relationships are fraught with conflict, you may find yourself dreading going home at the end of a long, stressful day.

The amount of stress we experience from family life also depends on how demanding our roles are at any particular time in our lives. For example, if you're a new parent with a demanding infant, you may find that when your alarm goes off in the morning you feel as though you just can't keep going. Or maybe you're caring for a parent with dementia, or your romantic relationship may be going through a difficult time and you're not sure if you're going to last over the long haul.

Toxic Relationships

Although friends and family can provide lots of support when we are going through trying times, sometimes it is these problematic relationships themselves that are the source of our stress. If you find that certain relationships make you feel drained and overwhelmed, sad, or frustrated every time you engage, then perhaps it's time to rethink the relationship. Being around people you love is supposed to make you feel good, loved, cared about, and supported, no matter what. Loving difficult people is hard; you don't have to stop loving them, but you don't have to perpetually feel bad because of them. Setting emotional boundaries for yourself will make you less stressed even as you mourn what you wish the relationship could be but clearly isn't. For more on setting boundaries, see Learn to Say No, here.

Health

Stress and health are two issues that go hand in hand. People who experience a lot of stress may have related illnesses such as hypertension or cardiovascular disease. Stress also manifests itself in physical issues like hair loss, skin problems, asthma, and panic attacks.

Social Media and Technology

The negative impact of social media is connected to our constant need to compare ourselves to other people. The problem is that on social media, friends, family, and influencers only show the best parts of their lives. Social media is also a distraction from work, and for some of us—including me—it is easy to get sucked down the rabbit hole when we have more important things to do.

Research has shown that we touch our phones thousands of times a day. Even if you are not connected to social media, your mobile devices keep you constantly connected to the world of work. You may check your e-mail at night and feel compelled to respond as soon as you can. Many people check and respond to their e-mail while on vacation because they're afraid that if they don't, their inboxes will be overflowing when they return to work. Technology often means that we are always reachable. This is why some companies have taken steps to shut down servers on weekends or after hours so that workers can disconnect, take a break, and be more productive when they are actually at work.

But it's not just work that keeps us on a leash. Even our cars come with the ability to connect to the Internet and to our phones, leaving us no place to hide and no time to ourselves.

Ask yourself why social media and technology are stressful for you and record your observations below.

Major Life Changes

Major shifts in our lives cause stress because change is stressful, even if it is necessary or wanted. Major life changes such as the birth of a child, a marriage, moving to another city, or a change in employment can create a disruption in our lives that requires us to reinvent ourselves in some way. If you move to another city, you have to find a new salon, a new gym, and the shortest or fastest way to work. You need to find a new favorite restaurant and a new route to run or walk. If you have a new job, you have to learn the new office politics and get used to a new boss, new tasks, and new work relationships. Planning a marriage or preparing for a new member of the family can be very stressful, even though these events are a source of happiness. The same goes for sending a child off to college. You are happy for your child, but now you may have a little too much free time to manage.

Loss

Whether it is the loss of a relationship or a loved one, these life changes require us to think for a long period of time about our identity or mortality. Yes, we know that we are all going to die, but losing someone who means something to us often makes us reconsider who we are and what we want out of life. Even if the loss is something that we wanted, like the end of a bad relationship, we still experience stress as we try to reorient our lives to accommodate a new role. Loss is particularly stressful because we may feel like we can't address the person who is gone.

Environment and Surroundings

The environment where we live, and work can be a source of stress. Even for those of us who love living in cities, the density, concrete, pollution, and noise can put us on edge. This is why people often seek out green spaces, like rooftop gardens, to feel relaxed. Living in a neighborhood where you don't feel safe or living next to a noisy neighbor can also be a source of stress. Sometimes, where we live is a source of stress because we live in areas that are very socially competitive. No matter what your worries are, write them out so you can understand them better.

Internal Stressors

In addition to the external causes of stress, some of the stressors in our lives are internal. These include our fears, such as the fear of flying, fear of public speaking, or fear about how we are viewed in social settings. Sometimes we experience stress because we don't feel as though we're in control, whether regarding the outcome of a medical test or the traffic jam on the way home from work. Beliefs about and expectations of we can cause stress, too. Maybe you believe you're on the outs with your family when you're not, or you may expect that you should have a perfect life, which isn't possible.

Chapter 3 How Stress Develop and Transform to Anxiety

I t is fascinating to learn that our thoughts define what happens to us. From a psychological perspective, it means that we can control what happens to us by simply learning how to control our thoughts. This is a powerful technique indeed. Knowing that you have power over what happens to you is something that most people are unaware of. The reality is that you become what you think. If you look closely, whatever happens to you, good or bad, stems from your thoughts.

What you think about affects your mental health and wellbeing. Your thoughts lead to the emotional state that you might be experiencing. Often, this will affect your health. If your thoughts are preoccupied with sad events, then chances are that you will constantly feel sad. If you are constantly thinking about the fun activities that you engage in with your friends, then you attract the same energy to your life. From this, you will garner deeper insight into why your thoughts could be identified as the cause for your dwindling productivity at work, lack of sleep and your failing social relationships.

Your thoughts and feelings will work together to build an ideal future for yourself. Since you have the power to decide what you want, you ought to request a life that you've always dreamt of living. Your focus and energy should be in line with what you want to attract.

After understanding the fact that you are the creator of your world, you should begin thinking consciously towards creating a better life for yourself. In this case, this should encourage you to think positively since your thoughts define what you want in life. This requires that you channel your time and energy on thinking about the good things you want in life. It also means that you should deliberately manage your thoughts and emotions as they have an impact on what manifests.

Anxiety: Stopping Negative Thoughts

Anxiety is caused by numerous factors. At times, it is caused by a combination of genetic factors and environmental factors. Fear within you can easily make you feel worried about things that haven't happened. In extreme cases, this leads to panic. Your mind can easily amplify the fears within you and make you believe that something bad will happen. In social settings, anxiety will leave you in a constant state of worry of saying the wrong thing in front of other people. Also, you might gain the assumption that other people will not like you. Such negative thoughts only prevent you from being yourself. It holds you back from living your life.

Stress

You could end up developing a fear of lose your job. Indeed, this will stress you out a lot. In some cases, stress harms the quality of your sleep. This worsens your situation as anxiety tends to worsen when you don't have enough sleep.

Negative thinking will often lead to stress. When you constantly dwell on negative self-talk, this is what your subconscious mind will focus on. Instead of ruminating on how bad things follow you, it is vital to realize that such thoughts can hurt your emotional wellbeing.

Stress and Negative Self-Talk

Self-talk is the inner voice that talks to you. Depending on how you use self-talk, it becomes a make-or-break situation. Positive self-talk will remind you of the great things that you can achieve. It will help you approach life with optimism. Negative self-talk, on the other hand, will attract negative energy. You will pay too much attention to the possibility of all the bad things that could happen to you. Negative self-talk will not help you overcome the stress that you might be going through. it worsens the situation as you will feel more stressed.

Overthinking can affect your life in many ways. Whether you are feeling anxious, stressed, or unmotivated, all these can be attributed to how you think. Your thoughts define who you are. Thinking positively can attract good things to you. The law of attraction will always apply to your thoughts and emotions. It is through these thoughts that you create the world that you want. Negative thinking breeds negativity in your life. It will affect your relationships, work-life, and your productivity in varying aspects. Instead of worrying about the future, you should use your energy to focus more on what you can do today for a better tomorrow. Frankly, your actions determine your future. Hence, thinking alone is just not enough. You need to act.

Overthinking is that inner voice that tries to bring you down. It criticizes you and destroys your confidence and self-esteem. You not only doubt yourself, but you also doubt those who are close to you. It pushes you to second guess everything. Thinking too much can be compared to a spreading fire. It burns down everything that it finds on its way. Therefore, you will suffer as a result of overthinking.

Overthinking is when your mind clings to the faults that you have made and takes you through them throughout the day. When you overthink, your life will be on constant pause. You will always feel as though you are waiting for the right moment to do something. The problem is that this moment never arrives. You're always anticipating that something could go wrong. You will be overly careful when doing anything. This is influenced by the fact that you are just worried things might not work out as expected.

Chapter 4 The Importance of Not Underestimating Stress

We yearn for a happy, peaceful, fulfilled life, but if we do not make conscious efforts to mitigate and manage our stress levels on a daily basis, we can never really have that life. You need to be truly motivated to address your chronic stress positively and regularly. Let me walk you through the various ways through which stress affects and sabotages your life so that you understand the dire need to tend to this issue seriously.

How Stress Affects Your Health, Wellbeing and Life?

Chronic stress takes a toll on your body, mind, sanity and every aspect of your life. It upsets, sabotages and disturbs your life in the following ways:

- Constantly staying in a state of stress disrupts your ability to stay focused and think clearly. When you are extremely disturbed, you ruminate on bad experiences and cannot pay attention to important tasks. This negatively affects your performance and productivity in tasks.

- Stress often makes you irritable and you lose your calm on even the most trivial issues. You find yourself yelling more often at your kids and loved ones and panicking at the slightest of disturbances.

- When you become a mere pressure cooker, people find it hard to be around you. they become distant from you and you miss out on valuable moments with loved ones.

- Feeling swamped and isolated from loved ones only upsets you more pushing you towards emotional disorders such as anxiety and depression.

- Moreover, when you perceive everything as stressful, you lose interest even in activities that once brought you happiness. Nothing brings you joy and meaning, and you start to sense a huge void in your life.

- Stress when it goes unchecked for long leads to physical problems such as constant headaches, shoulder pains, backaches, upset stomach, chest pain and insomnia. You feel more frustrated and find it difficult to live a comfortable life.

- In addition, stress is one of the most common root causes of high blood pressure, diabetes and heart problems. If you become prone to chronic stress, it is only a matter of time before you start struggling with these problems.

- Stress is also linked to six of the major causes of death: cancer, accidents, heart disease, lung ailments, suicide and live cirrhosis.

To sum it up, life only becomes more difficult and painful when stress becomes a constant in it.

Before moving on, here are a few preparatory measures and guidelines we would like you to understand.

Preparatory Tips and Measures to Practice Stress Management

- Firstly, understand that stress management is not a one-time thing. You need to practice all the measures taught on a daily basis to yield a strong, compound effect. For instance, taking deep breaths when you panic on having to meet a deadline definitely calms you down. However, if you do not make a conscious effort to breathe deeply regularly, you are likely to panic again the next time. Remember to observe all the measures and strategies on a regular basis to gradually equip yourself with the ability to keep stress at bay at all times.

- Wrap your head around the fact that no matter how hard you try; some amount of stress will always affect you. It is inevitable so you need to stop trying to completely eradicate stress from your life and focus primarily on becoming strong enough to address it positively.

- Take your time and read one at a time. Go through it a couple of times, analyze the teachings and then practically apply them in your life. If you are asked to avoid seeing people who trigger your stress, you need to actually do that and observe the effects of this strategy. Remember, only practical and real-life application of strategies yields desired results; reading and accepting them alone would not do the trick.

- Keep a small pocketsize notebook with you at all times to record your stress management journey. When you start working on a certain strategy, note down how you feel about yourself and your life at that moment along with your stress levels. Once you have actually carried out a certain measure, observe your feelings and stress levels again, and write them down. If your stress levels have even dropped down a little, it shows the trick is working and you need to continue with it to gradually mitigate your stress better. Also, analyze how well or poorly, you carried out that strategy to become better aware of your strengths and weaknesses. If you are told to practice gratitude throughout the day, but you kept reminiscing bad memories instead of counting your blessings, that is a weakness you need to improve on. This journal helps you keep track of your performance, pinpoint your mistakes and strengths, and gives you an understanding of areas of improvement. If you follow it strictly, you will soon have your thoughts and stress levels under control.

These guidelines if observed regularly help you move closer to your goal; a stress-free, happy and meaningful life. Now that we have covered the basics, let us move on to the first step of stress management.

Chapter 5 Difference Between Overthinking and Anxiety

The two terms are often used interchangeably, and since many of the symptoms tend to overlap, it's understandable to see why. While they share many similar traits, anxiety is a completely different matter altogether. From the symptoms we experience to the way we experience, one of the few common similarities overthinking and anxiety shares are the havoc they wreak on our psychological and emotional health. What are these subtle yet important distinctions between the two? Let's find out.

Anxiety is identified by the following characteristics:

- Originally, anxiety is a survival mechanism present in all of us. Its primary function is to alert us to the presence of danger, and it is not meant to be an emotion that lingers for long. Once the danger has passed, anxiety should dissipate, but that's not the case if you happen to be dealing with an anxiety disorder.

- Activates the body's fight or flight response.

- With an anxiety disorder, the body remains in an unnatural heightened state of alertness. Everything feels like a cause for alarm, and it triggers a constant flow of cortisol throughout the body.

- Diagnosed as a psychiatric or mental health disorder that is capable of derailing your daily life because of the persistent fear and worry that seems to follow you everywhere you go.

- It does not necessarily originate from a logical source, making it difficult to pinpoint what the underlying cause may be. It can be difficult to talk yourself out of an anxious episode.

- It has a stigma associated with it because it is classified as a mental health issue. It is not uncommon for those struggling with anxiety to be misunderstood, even by those who are closest to them.

- It can feel like a lonely and isolating burden to bear when you feel disconnected to the people closest to you. Many who struggle with anxiety are often embarrassed to admit what they're going through out of fear of being rejected.

- The anxious thoughts manifest differently from one person to the next.

- Anxiety tends to make you feel like you're running in a hamster wheel, going round and round in circles with no productive solution or end in sight.

- The emotions, fear, panic, and distress felt can make it feel impossible to function normally in your routine. Some people experience anxiety to such an extreme level they're too afraid to leave the house, let alone do anything else that requires venturing outside their comfortable or "safe" zone.

- Relentless and persistent worries that won't seem to go away, no matter how hard the person may try to reason with themselves. The fear felt can sometimes be so great that it leads to a panic attack episode.

- Insomnia and difficulty are trying to stay calm in a lot of situations.

- Irritable, frustrated, tired, and feeling like they are always on edge are some of the common emotions felt by those dealing with this disorder.

- The physical symptoms that are associated with this condition include shortness of breath, difficulty breathing, rapid heartbeat, sweaty palms, upset stomach, difficulty concentrating, and muscle aches and pains.

- A persistent sense of foreboding or dread, like something bad, is going to happen at any time.

- Some instances of severe anxiety may require medical intervention or treatment to help resolve the situation.

Overthinking, on the other hand, is associated with the following traits:

- Originally meant to be used as a method to resolve. When experienced in excess, overthinking disrupts our ability to think rationally and logically.

- Part of the usual thought process cycle for many people.

- Situations, events, or thoughts can cause immense stress and a lot of unnecessary worries. However, the concerns tend to be a lot more realistic than those of anxiety.

- A source or trigger is almost always immediately identifiable. Since the worrying thought stems from something specific, you may be able to talk yourself out of it and calm your thoughts.

- Overthinking is mostly a mental experience, unlike anxiety, where the symptoms are severe enough to manifest physically. With overthinking, we tend to be caught up in our thoughts more so than anything else.

- Less likely to produce a strong cardiovascular response the way anxiety does.

- In some cases, overthinking could trigger problem-solving and acts as a strong enough motivator that gets you actively thinking about the solutions, so you don't have to deal with the problem any longer.

- The emotional distress felt is a lot milder than what you would experience with anxiety. Aside from impeding your ability to focus, overthinking is less likely to cause any real problems to your ability to function in your daily routine.

- Overthinking is a condition that is a lot more manageable than its anxious counterpart. Since overthinking has the potential to lead to problem-solving, every solution you come up with means your worry diminishes your worries a little bit more.

- The worries experience here can either be temporary, or they can linger longer than they should. Generally, once a problem has been resolved, the mind should be put at ease and move on to something else to focus on.

- Less likely to impact our professional and personal lives the way anxiety would. Overthinking does not have the same stigma associated with it the way anxiety does.

- Worrying and the tendency to overthink is still considered a normal psychological state, unlike anxiety. However, overthinking excessively is not healthy either.

- It does not require medication to treat the condition.

Almost similar yet subtly different. Anxiety and overthinking are neither healthy nor helpful. The anxious brain is not an easy entity to deal with. It's hypervigilant and always on alert for anything that might be perceived as dangerous or a threat. The fight or flight response is the body's primal mechanism for protecting itself against danger. It is what the earliest humans used to help them survive and thrive when the living conditions were a lot more dangerous than what they are today. This response is also referred to as acute stress response, and it shares the same reactions or feelings, such as shaking anxiety and fear that occurs when our body is preparing for a possible emergency. The term fight or flight first started going around sometime in the 1920s as the first part of involuntary general adaptation syndrome.

Our fight-or-flight response is a reaction to stress, and this is a reaction that most likely evolved out of the survival needs from our early ancestors who lived in dangerous times. For example, prehistoric cavemen were in constant danger of animals. One minute they might be lighting a fire, and the next minute, there's a stampede coming their way, and they need to evacuate as soon as possible. The human body's natural survival design then kicks in and we have a full surge of energy and strength to quickly respond to the threat by removing ourselves from danger and increasing our chances of survival. Numerous physiological changes have been identified by researchers that happen when the flight-or-fight response takes place. It is believed that these changes are triggered by the sympathetic nervous system that is released through stress hormones into our bodies. When this happens, it causes a quick and instant physical reaction in preparation of the muscular activity that is required to fight or flee the danger. However, the body is not meant to remain in this state of alertness for long. All that cortisol pumping through your body will eventually take its toll on your mental, physical and emotional health.

When anxiety is thrown into the mix, our brains are churning out an endless stream of worried thoughts that never seem to end. Day and night, and even when we're trying to go to sleep at night, these thoughts won't leave us alone. We never seem to have a moment's rest, and we can't remember what it was like to feel relaxed anymore. Since these thoughts seem to be relentless and go on for a prolonged period, we eventually run the risk of believing what the mind is trying to tell us. That's dangerous territory to venture into. After all, if your thoughts have the power to shape your reality, then everything you allow yourself to believe is going to manifest one way or another. The good news is, neither of these conditions needs to be part of our permanent existence for long.

Chapter 6 What Causes Mental Clutter?

W hat comes into your mind when you hear of mental clutter? Do you visualize a physical clutter that you know of? Mental clutter simply means mental overload, mental stress or mental fatigue. This is anything that gives you anxiety, depression, frustration, sense of overwhelm, and anger. This clutter comes in the form of:

- Regrets for past failures and regret for not doing some things that you should have done

- Too many bills to pay and increasing debts as well as unfinished projects

- Worries and insecurities

- Inner critic

- Feeling bad for failing to achieve something

These thoughts hinder us from focusing and working to improve ourselves. They divert our thoughts to the past instead of focusing on now and tomorrow. Mental clutter occupies our mental space, messes with our minds, eliminates our mental clarity and it is bad for our mental health.

What Causes Mental Clutter

1. Worry

When we encounter challenges in our daily activities, our brains naturally go to a state of worry. Although it is a natural reaction, we can always control it because it will not solve any of our problems. Instead, worrying will worsen the situation. Worrying will take away your peace of mind and it will stress you. Worrying is a waste of energy.

The best thing you can do is to stop worrying. Find something to do that will divert your thoughts to something better like going for a walk, dancing, cooking or anything that interests you. You can also write down those things that are robbing you of your peace of mind and write how you are going to solve them.

2. Regret

Gee whiz! "I wish I worked hard in school my life could be better!" Such remarks are common when having a conversation with friends or family members. We all have those things we wish we had done or not done in our lives! Sometimes our minds can focus on those things, but we should not allow it. Focusing your minds on regrets will rob you of your happiness and cause you mental fatigue and stress. You cannot change the past so put your energy into creating a better vision for your life.

3. Fear

Fear is an enemy of progress! You should not allow fear to hinder you from taking chances and chasing after your dreams and enjoying life.

Do you dream of owning a business, but you are afraid that it might not take off if you start? Start it anyway and silence the fear that you have.

4. Guilt and shame

We should take responsibility for our wrongdoings and learn some lessons from it. Never allow yourself to be a prisoner of guilt and shame because it will cause you to have resentment self-hate, and even kill your self-esteem. The best way to get rid of guilt and shame is to acknowledge your mistake, forgive yourself and move on. This will empower you, motivate you to become a better person, make you value yourself. You should never repeat the same mistake.

5. The inner critic

How do you perceive yourself? Do you frequently have negative self-talk dominating your mind? Negative self-talk will limit our mental growth and lower our self-confidence. Remember your brain will believe what you tell it. If you constantly tell yourself that you cannot do it, your brain will act according to that belief.

You need to learn to refuse negative self-talk and replace it with positive talk. If the inner critic is telling you that you cannot do it then do it and you will silence that inner critic that is hindering your progress in life. Talk to yourself positively every day and you will see changes and your self-confidence and esteem will improve making you feel good about yourself.

The Negative Effects of Mental Clutter

1. Clutter is not good for your health

Research has shown that mental clutter can harm your health and physical wellbeing. This is because of the following reasons:

- It increases your stress levels

When you have an endless list of unfinished projects, unpaid bills, and debts, it can lead to stress. Mental clutter will stress the brain and it will release a stress hormone cortisol. This can lead to some undesirable health conditions like chronic stress, high blood pressure, slow digestion, poor sleeping habits, and depression that can cause mental illness.

Stress will exhaust your mental energy leaving you feeling tired and overwhelmed. It will also make you lose focus and concentration on important things and it promotes negative self-talk.

- It interferes with your eating habits

Mental clutter can make you lose appetite or crave for more unhealthy food because of the rise of stress levels. Research has shown that people with mental clutter eat twice as many cookies, sweets, and snacks than those people who do not suffer from mental clutter. That means when you have a mental clutter you will not prioritize a healthy diet, but you will crave junk food, which is unhealthy, and it can make you fat.

2. It steals your productivity

Mental clutter promotes stress and anxiety that will suck your energy making you feel lazy, unproductive, and useless. Clutter will distract your focus because so many things are fighting for your attention and this can affect your productivity. Having an endless "to-do" list can be hard to handle and it can make you feel like you are losing your mind. This feeling of never completing projects will ground your mind and it will create negative self-talk that can hinder your progress.

When your mind is full of clutter, you may find that you do not remember where you put certain files then you spend so much time looking for those work files. These can delay your work, you may fail to meet deadlines, and this may make you feel like giving up.

3. Less efficient thinking

Mental clutter will prevent you from processing important information. It can also lead to temporary memory loss. Mental clutter will take away your focus leaving you confused with endless "to-do" tasks. Such overwhelming feelings will render you helpless and you may find that even doing a small task is difficult. It can also affect your parenting styles negatively because you will project your anger and frustration on the children and that is not good for their mental growth.

4. It interferes with your relationships

Mental clutter will consume your energy and you will not have the energy to give your loved ones. You can't give full attention to the people you love when your mind is full of clutter because mental clutter is distracting since there is so much stuff fighting for your attention in your mind. The inability to give the people you love your attention and energy will make them suffer.

Clutter will give you stress, and mental fatigue and you will feel overwhelmed from the pile-up of things that needs your attention as a result, you will project some frustration onto your loved ones. Although you will be doing this unknowingly it will affect your relationships negatively because you will be moody and resentful most of the time. You might end up treating them harshly and they may develop a negative attitude towards you.

Mental clutter may isolate you from other people. Since you will be feeling stressed out and mentally tired, you may not want to interact with other people because their presence will irritate you. If you have children, your mental clutter will not allow you to have a good time with them and this will affect them psychologically because they will feel like you do not value them. Such children may suffer from unhappiness, anxiety, and they may have difficulties in socializing with their peers.

5. It will rob you of your peace of mind

Your mind can never relax if you are suffering from mental clutter. It will always be wandering! This will leave you with stress, frustration, discontent, and these feelings can be overwhelming to your mind. Find something that can help you decongest your mind and relax. You can listen to soothing music, meditate or take a walk in the park, anything that will relieve your mental clutter.

6. It can lead to procrastination

Since mental clutter will drain your energy, you will end up postponing some tasks because of mental fatigue and stress. The best way to stop procrastination is by clearing your mind of unnecessary thoughts so that it can focus on doing important things that can make you a better person.

7. It will keep you in the past

When your mind is full of clutter, you will not be able to receive new ideas because there is not any room left for them. Your life will only be revolving around the clutter in your mind that are normally worries from past events and uncertainty of the future. Whining about your past situations will derail you from achieving a better tomorrow. So, let go of your past and have a clear plan of how you can achieve your aspirations and goals in life.

8. It affects your emotions

There is no way you can be happy with mental clutter. It will bring you feelings of anger, sadness, discontent and it will be hard for you to have positive feelings like being happy, confident or proud. The mental clutter will spike your stress hormones giving you dull feelings every day!

9. Encourages bad money management

Mental clutter can cause you to have surprise bills because you may have forgotten to pay them. The clutter in your mind may make you forget to pay bills on time, and this can cause you to pay some penalty fee. It can also cause you to have bad credits. You may also find yourself buying stuff that you already have but you cannot remember. Mental clutter can also make you forget to keep count of how much money you use per week or month and this will make you a poor financial manager.

10. It will derail your career and prevent you from getting promoted

When you lose focus and concentration in your work, you become less productive and this is not healthy for your career. Most managers demand performance in the workplace, and you cannot keep up with that if you have mental clutter. If you want to be successful in your career, you need to clear your mind and focus on doing your best in everything you do.

Chapter 7 Decluttering Your Mind

You must declutter your mind; it is essential to your mental health, productivity, and ability to concentrate. If you have a cluttered mind, you may struggle to sleep at night. You won't be able to focus on work. It will be difficult to enjoy your life when you are weighed down with countless thoughts and filled with worries. There are a few ways that you can work on decluttering your mind.

One way to declutter your mind is to declutter your physical space. You may be mentally overwhelmed because of the physical environment that you are in. If your workspace is unorganized and filled with junk, your mind will reflect that; you won't be able to focus on your work. For this reason, it's necessary to go through your space and get rid of anything that you don't need. This will allow you to focus on what's important. Your home, workspace, and car will all influence your mental health. Put yourself in an environment that helps you to focus instead of distracting you from focusing.

Another way to declutter your mind is learning how to not multi-task. It is instinctual to multi-task, as it seems like a way of getting more done. However, you are splitting your focus among several tasks instead of giving your total focus to one. This will result in work that is of a lower quality, and you will feel overwhelmed as a result. Start making it a habit to completely finish one task before moving onto another. You will notice a dramatic change for doing so, as you will accomplish more and feel better about your work.

You can also declutter the number of decisions that you must make. You may also prepare ahead of time so that you feel better when it actually happens. For instance, you may plan your outfits for the entire week on Sunday night. You may meal-prep so that you don't have to worry about food when it's mealtime. Make a schedule for routine tasks you must complete, such as doing laundry every Thursday morning or vacuuming every Wednesday night. Reducing your decisions and coming up with a schedule can really help you to stop overthinking and have a schedule that you already know works for you. You may make a schedule for yourself so that you know exactly what to do.

Sunday	Monday	Tuesday	Wednesday	Thursday	Friday	Saturday
Pick clothes	Bathroom	Dishes	Vacuum	Laundry	Trash	Meal-prep

Minimalism

Minimalism isn't simply getting rid of things or decluttering your belongings. It is seeing what truly matters to you and sticking with that. Marie Kondo's method is to only keep items that "spark joy." This means that you only keep the items in your life that truly make you happy. It can really help you to go through each item that you own and decide what matters to you. You may have some things that you keep out of guilt or for "someday in the future." However, these items will only disappoint and frustrate you each time you see them. It is important to eliminate any items that bring you negativity or remind you of failure. Surround yourself with items that bring you joy and make you a better person. Your surroundings should be a reflection of you and what you love. You may choose to go through the items in your house, at work, in your car, and any other places that you may have. Do not bring any other items into your life that bring you down in any way; only own what you truly need to make you happy. This can help you to have a much clearer mind.

Learning to Focus

Take some time to reflect on where you stand with your focus. Are you happy with your ability to focus? Do you wish that your focus could be improved? Figure out what your goal is. Do you find yourself getting distracted easily, unable to continue work after taking a break, or simply can't finish tasks with ease? Determine what it is that prevents you from focusing.

You may try to challenge yourself. Give yourself a task and a time limit and do your best. Become aware of how often you become distracted and how easily you can regain your focus. Write down anything that distracts you; you may not even realize how distracted you become! Afterward, ensure that you rid yourself of any distractions. Turn off your notifications. Make sure that it's quiet and peaceful. Whatever distracts you, make sure it's eliminated. You may also come up with a schedule for your breaks. Figure out what works best for you. Perhaps you like to work for fifty minutes and take a ten-minute break. Perhaps you prefer to work longer and have a longer break. It will depend on your personal preference. Regardless, it's important to remain completely focused while you are working and to also take breaks regularly. This will increase your productivity and allow you to be less stressed. Determine what sets you off. What is it that makes you lose your focus? Why do you overthink? Reflecting can really help you to determine the causes of your actions.

Overall, it's important to take care of your mental health so that you can focus better. By taking some time to yourself and doing small things that you love, you can really help yourself to feel better. When you are happy, you will feel much more motivated and find it much easier to focus.

Prioritizing

Perhaps you are able to focus, but you simply aren't focusing on what you should. It can be quite easy to get caught up in tasks that are unimportant or aren't urgent. You may think that you're being productive, but you're really procrastinating. This is why prioritizing is so important. You must be able to recognize where you should be placing your focus. Otherwise, it's like you're on a treadmill. You're still getting something done, but you aren't actually going anywhere. You must learn to prioritize your tasks properly so that you focus first on what's important. After that, you may move on to other tasks.

One way to prioritize is by making to-do lists every day. It is helpful to make them the night before so that you can plan ahead of time. At the moment, you may not feel as motivated to accomplish every task. It helps to have one to three major tasks for the day. These are your top tasks. Even if they are the only things you accomplish for the day, you would be happy with yourself. These are your top priority, and it is what you should focus on accomplishing first. This will allow you to focus on what you must.

You should also write down any additional goals that you have for the day. Write every possible thing that is on your mind. Make a list of all of the potential tasks, even if they aren't necessary for the day. By doing a "brain dump," you are freeing yourself of clutter in your mind. This will really help you to focus on the present instead of the past or future. Additionally, you will feel better knowing that you won't forget anything that you would like to do. It will all be written down, so you can feel more at peace.

Decluttering your mind will help you to remove all of your unnecessary thoughts. You will learn how to focus on what matters so that you may direct your energy towards that. Similarly, practicing minimalism will help you to understand what you value in life. You will realize what you should put your focus on, and what you find important. You can learn to focus by means of a few methods. Physical and mental health will play a huge role in your ability to focus. Finally, prioritizing will help you to learn what you should focus your attention on. You will feel more at ease when you can focus on what you need to.

Chapter 8 Declutter Your Physical Environment

Sometimes, we forget that living in an environment that is messy, cluttered, filthy and disorganized, can take its toll. There is no one out there who will tell you they like feeling overwhelmed. The word alone invokes feelings of unpleasantness, isolation, and failure. Almost like you feel disappointed with yourself for being unable to cope. That's the word you're going to be using a lot, though, if you live in the kind of environment that is described above. Walking into your garage, you can't find anything that you're looking for and it's a struggle to maneuver past the boxes and piles of stuff that are scattered all over the place. You open your drawers and there's a pile of items scattered in there you don't even use anymore. Doing a quick inventory of your home might surprise you with several items you don't recall buying. That's the thing about stuff. It tends to pile up and if you're like so many others out there, it's hard to let go.

Feeling "overwhelmed" by the clutter that surrounds our lives has become a common dirty little secret. Most of us go through it, but nobody likes to talk about it because talking about it means you've got to admit you have a clutter problem. A lot of us have this obsessive need to fill everything we have. We fill our houses, our cars, our offices, our workstations, our mobile phones, tablets, laptops, storage units, cupboards, shelves, and we fill both our minds and our hearts with unnecessary clutter. It's more than we can manage, and it's no wonder we feel as overwhelmed as we do. Why do we continuously keep taking more? Because we believe "more" will lead to happiness. We believe if we buy the latest mobile phone, we're going to be happy. If we buy the newest car on the market, we're going to be happy. A new watch, a new pair of jeans, shoes, items for the home. Advertisements and commercials often portray a feeling of happiness when we purchase their product or engage in their services. Does retail therapy really make us happy? On some level, it does, but it's not the kind of happiness that lasts for long.

We keep buying and collecting believing with each new purchase that it's going to finally make us happy. In reality, all it does is perpetuate the overwhelming feeling we already have. The words "clutter", "decluttering" and "minimalism" has exploded in today's society because this is a very real problem. We know by now that clutter is not limited to the physical belongings that clog up our space, it could be digital, mental, spiritual, and emotional. The physical clutter is the one our minds automatically go to when we hear the term "clutter". To tackle the other aspects of a cluttered life, you need to work on the physical and the rest will gradually fall into place. When your life is simpler, your brain automatically becomes less cluttered. Coming home to a space that is neat, organized, and with plenty of room to move around is a breath of fresh air after the noisy outside world you left behind when you walked in the front door.

Your House Is a Container

We certainly treat it that way. Yes, we need to accept that our homes are a container. It's where we keep everything that we own. What we need to learn how to do now is to stop the overabundance. Messiness, even the minor ones, eventually takes its toll. It may not seem like a small pile of stuff here and there scattered haphazardly around your home is going to cause any real damage, but every type of clutter demands your attention. It might not be conscious or mindful attention, but your brain is still processing these stimuli whether you're paying attention or not.

Your home is a container, and it happens to be one container you spend a lot of time in when you're not at work. If this environment is constantly going to overwhelm your brain, you'll find it increasingly difficult to focus, make decisions, and the mental fatigue is going to leave you feeling exhausted and drained of energy all the time. In the pursuit of keeping up with this constant, on-the-go and hectic lifestyle, we have forgotten that there are other aspects of our life that need looking after. Our health, relationships, personal growth, and mental health have taken a backseat as we race for what else we can buy, who has what new item and finding reasons to constantly make new and unnecessary purchases we don't need. We have become far too consumeristic and materialistic, and it is time to change all of that.

A home should be a space you look forward to coming back to each day. A space that makes you happy, lifts your mood and elevates your spirits. It should be your sanctuary, not a place that fills you with even more stress. To create such an environment, you need to accomplish two goals:

- Simplicity for Greater Clarity - Get rid of anything that is unnecessary, that's the rule of thumb for simplicity. If you don't need it, then toss it (or donate it). One study done by Princeton University reveals that cleaning up the environment within your immediate field of vision can help prevent your brain from overloading. Without the brain fog, it becomes a lot easier to think clearly.

- Break Away from Boredom - As much as we need routine, after a while it can become boring. When it does, you lose motivation and any desire to get things done. The American Psychological Association believes that the reason you feel bored could be because what you're doing now lacks purpose. Meaning there are steps in your daily routine or environment that don't make you feel happy or fulfilled. Research done on this subject indicates that a change in your environment, even if it is a slight shift, might be what you need to change your outlook and get a different perspective on life. If your work desk is cluttered and makes you feel uninspired, clearing it out and leaving nothing more than your laptop and a notepad on it can leave you feeling rejuvenated. Your brain is processing this as something new, and that sparks excitement. It's been a while since it saw a desk this empty and simplistic, and that change wakes the brain up, renewing your sense of purpose while it's at it.

Valuing Space Over Stuff

Space is an asset that is underrated. We put so much value on our material belongings that we forget the space we have is limited. There's only so much your home, car, desk, garage, closet, and drawers can handle before it's packed to the brim. Yet, we can't seem to bring ourselves to stop buying. Space is no longer considered "space" when there's no room to move around anymore. Have you ever felt that there was no room to breathe? Claustrophobic? Trapped? Confined, perhaps? That's your brain trying to signal to you that there is too much going on. Now, compare those feelings to the way you feel after you've done a little spring cleaning. Do you breathe a sigh of relief? Immediately feel lighter. Better? If we learn how to place value on the precious space we have, then perhaps we wouldn't be so quick to fill it up again as soon as we've made some room.

The benefits of valuing your space and decluttering go beyond trying to make your home look like something out of a Pinterest board. It's the mental, physical, emotional and even financial benefits that you gain which makes this process worthwhile. Understandably, the thought of getting rid of most of what you have accumulated over the years can be daunting. Some people have a very strong emotional attachment to certain possessions that they own, even if they may not have used or touched those items in years. The question of "What if I need this?" is always going to linger at the back of your mind. But ask yourself this: Is the mess worth your stress?

We all have different battles we're fighting with clutter. Some are more physical, while others could be more emotional or mental. But once you start valuing your space, you're going to see the following changes unfold:

- You Feel a Greater Sense of Relief - Clearing away the clutter in your life is going to feel like a big weight has been lifted off your shoulders. Suddenly, you have room to breathe again once more. We often don't realize just how much we are affected by the clutter and accumulation of possessions around us until we get rid of it and feel much better when we've tossed out a few items.

- You're Clearer About What You Don't Want - As you methodically work through your items, you'll start to realize which are the ones you value the most. Gaining clarity of what you don't want simultaneously creates clarity about the things you do want. Decluttering seems like a simple enough exercise in clarity, but the ability to separate what you want from the things you don't want will carry over into other areas of your life too.

- You Feel Motivated Again - There's an added benefit to being able to clearly identify what you want and what you don't. Your motivation is reawakened, thanks to the newfound, clearer purpose in your life. Without the unnecessary distractions taking away your focus, you are once again able to see your purpose, remember what your goals are and what you want to accomplish.

- You're A Lot More Efficient - You are able to concentrate better, your priorities more in focus, you find yourself feeling lighter, happier, and able to work a lot more efficiently and make more productive use of your time because you have fewer things around you that distract you.

- Less Stress Means Better Mental Health - Greater focus and clarity reminds you of what you have been neglecting all along. That you matter more than any material possessions you could possibly buy. The moment you start focusing on yourself again, your mental and physical health starts to shine because you're working on becoming a better you. If you continued to live with stress, none of this would be possible.

Chapter 9 Overthinking and Its Causes

What exactly is overthinking? Experts overview overthinking syndrome as spending much of your time thinking of anything and something which causes stress, fear, restlessness, concern, dread, unease, and many others. This mental condition is not just about too much thinking of something, but also about spending more thoughts, which affects the capability of the person to work and finish the daily tasks.

If you worry about your friends, your job, your family, your boyfriend, and girlfriend, your life and anything else; You believe that you do not have overthinking condition; No matter what you are thinking about, perhaps concerns you for a moment, then a short span of time, you continue with other parts of your life. Yes, you return wondering every so often. However, you do not continuously wonder, and you do not find it getting in the way with the rest of your life. With this kind of mental condition, however, the troubled is all that you can think of. Even if you may not be troubled on the same thing regularly and repeatedly, you always worried about something.

No two individuals will suffer from this kind of mental issue in the same way. But people who do suffer overthinking will find that their daily living and lifestyle is at stake. This is due to their lack of capability of efficiently and successfully controlling negative thoughts as well as emotion. Thus, they find it hard to hang out and socialize. They also find it hard to enjoy their sidelines and hobbies. They are not helpful and not creative at work. All these happen since their mind spends an inconsistent amount of energy and time on particular lines of thoughts. There is a feeling that they do not have complete power over their emotions or minds that can be extremely destructive to mental wellbeing.

Making friends, meeting up with someone as well as keeping friends is hard with this mental condition as you resist interacting with them. You will experience difficulty in talking to the people that surrounds you. This happens because you are too much trouble with the things you do or say. You are also too much concerned about what will happen or how you will do it. If you, your friends or any member of the family experience, this mental disorder might struggle to make general conversation with others. It will also be hard to interrelate in a typical setting. You might find it so hard to go out to the department store or to your appointment, which affects your whole life in general.

Do you worry too much, even on simple things? Are you an extreme worrier? Maybe you automatically think that when you wonder/worry enough, you are able to avoid bad things from taking place. However, the reality is that worrying, and wondering are able to affect your system in so many ways which might astound you. If you think too much on everything or if you have excessive worrying, it can result in feelings of high stress and even lead to a serious health condition.

Causes of Overthinking

There is always a reason or a cause behind everything that happens. This includes the thoughts you have. Very rarely do thoughts randomly spring to mind for no apparent reason. When you catch yourself overthinking, there is always going to be a reason behind it. Something that sparked that train of thought. It is now up to you to identify what those triggers are. Now, this may be something you're reluctant or hesitant to do at first, but it needs to be done, nonetheless. It is important to identify your causes. Only when you know the root cause of any problem can you then begin to fix it. You're not alone. Excessive thoughts are something a lot of people struggle with each day. Let's look at some of the common excessive thinking triggers:

Trigger #1: Social Media

Social media usage has skyrocketed within the last decade. We spend more time on platforms like Facebook, Twitter, Instagram, and Snapchat more than we do on any other online space. What do you do when you find yourself idle or with some free time on your hands? Whether we like to admit it or not, social media is changing why and how we do certain things. It is even changing the way we think and has become one of the many triggers for the tendency to overthink. Why? Because when we're on social media, we start comparing.

We compare the life we have to the ones we see on social media. We compare our lives to that of our family and friends who seem to be having it all. Someone just got engaged. Someone's celebrating an anniversary. Someone else is about to jet off on a holiday you've been dying to go on. Someone just got promoted. When you look at all these, it becomes almost impossible not to compare. You look at all the smiling faces and enthusiastic announcements and start to think: Why not me? Why do they seem to have it all? Why can't I get that lucky? Why does my life have to be this way? It's no wonder social media usage has been linked to higher levels of depression on loneliness. An entire generation is growing up with lower self-esteem levels than the past generation. As if that wasn't worrying enough, they're growing up with higher levels of anxiety and a penchant for excessive thinking. They don't want to be obsessed with their thoughts, but they can't seem to help it.

Trigger #2: Relationship Anxiety

There could be several reasons why relationships might become a trigger for your excessive thoughts and anxiety. It could be a bad dating experience you had in the past that left you scarred to this day. Perhaps you struggle with insecurity and low self-esteem. Maybe you're afraid to open yourself up to your partner and expose the vulnerable side of yourself out of fear of getting hurt. Even the fear of getting hurt could send your thoughts and emotions hurtling out of control. Here's the interesting bit: People who struggle with relationship anxiety would STILL rather be in a relationship than be alone. Yet, when they become intimately involved with someone, the anxiety rears its ugly head and sabotages the relationship, thanks to all the overthinking and doubt, insecurities, and fears that are present. Without any way of controlling your thoughts or emotions, they can quickly get out of control, and it won't be long before you end up pushing your partner away.

Trigger #3: Living Up to Expectations

The fear of not living up to other people's expectations is a fear that haunts many anxiety-ridden overthinkers. When you spend too much time caring about what other people might do, say or think about you, you're not spending enough time caring about your happiness. Trying to live up to someone else's expectations prevents you from being fully present in your life. Why? Because the things you do are not done for you. You're not making decisions based on what's going to move you forward in life. You're not making decisions based on what's best for you. You're not investing time in tasks that are going to contribute to your future success.

Trigger #4: Worrying About Life in General

You worry about work, money, your family, the future, being stuck with an illness, school, your job, and the list could go on. Worrying about life, in general, is a big cause of overthinking, and it's no surprise either since there seems to be so much to worry about in the first place. We're worried all the time despite trying to paste a smile on our faces and present a calm, composed facade to the rest of the world. Overthinking in this category can feel pretty unbearable at times.

Your anxious excessive thoughts are often about specific or particular things, and most of the time, these excessive thoughts roam free in your mind when self-awareness is not present. Without self-awareness, it becomes difficult to see just how little control you have over the contents of your mind if you continue to allow overthinking to be the dominant force. The biggest trigger of anxious and excessive thoughts in this category is the fear of what we cannot control and the fear of what the future holds. Every facet of your life is going to bring with it some form of worry or another, and if you gave in to each of these thoughts, it could spell emotional disaster. Given the sheer number of things that could go wrong, indulging your overthinking mind is going to skyrocket your anxiety faster than you can keep up.

The human brain hates uncertainty. It doesn't take kindly to unknown variables and any element that is out of its control. That's why worrying about life, in general, is a major cause of overthinking. This is why anxiety sufferers and overthinkers find the prospect of the future so alarming. The fear of the unknown happens to be all the fuel their brain needs to start working overtime, churning out one negative thought after another.

Chapter 10 What are the Symptoms of Overthinking?

B
elow are symptoms that you are an overthinker:

When you talk fast

A person may appear to be nervous when they talk fast without pausing. However, this could be a sign that the person is an overthinker. A lot is usually happening inside an overthinker's mind. A person's mind may wander deep in thoughts, causing them to have a lot to say even though other people may not follow precisely what that person is talking about.

When you find yourself comparing people?

Sometimes overthinkers shift to a perfectionist mindset, and they start comparing other people and things to imagined standards of perfection. Such measures could come from Social Media and Media in general, where people make out everything to be perfect.

You Overanalyze Everything

If you notice that you overanalyze everything around you, then you are certainly an overthinker. This means that you may try to find a deeper meaning in all the experiences that you go through. When meeting new people, instead of engaging in productive communication, you may focus instead on how other people perceive you. Someone could be giving you a particular look and you may make several assumptions just based on that look. Overthinking consumes you. You end up wasting a lot of energy trying to figure out and make sense of the world around you. What you don't realize is that not everything has intrinsic meaning.

You Think Too Much but Don't Act

An overthinker will be affected by something called analysis paralysis. This is a scenario where you think too much about something but don't do anything about it in the end. In this case, you spend a lot of time weighing the options you have at your disposal. At first, you make up your mind on what the best alternative might be. Later, you compare your decision to other possible decisions that you could take. This means that you can't stop thinking about the possibilities and whether or not you made the right decision.

You Can't Let Go

Often, we make erroneous decisions that could lead us to fail. When this happens, it can be daunting to let go more so when you reflect on the sacrifices you have made to get to the point you are at. You might feel that it is painful to let go after you have invested a lot of money on a certain business.

You Always Want to Know Why

Without a doubt, the notion of asking why can be helpful to solve problems. This is because this probing attitude gets you the answers that you might be looking for. Nonetheless, it can also be damaging when you can't help but always wonder why. Overthinkers maintain such investigative attitude throughout their lives.

You Analyze People

The way you see other people can also say a lot about you. In most cases, you get lost thinking too much about how other people behave. You may tend to judge everybody that you come across. This one walks in a funny way. That person is not dressed well. You wonder what someone sitting at the park is smiling about. When these thoughts fill your head, you will only drain yourself. Spending too much time focusing on other people will only deter you from using your mind productively. Instead of visualizing your goals and your future, you waste your energy mulling over little things that add no value to you.

Regular Insomnia

Do you find it hard to sleep sometimes? You may get worked up over the idea that your brain cannot shut down and stop thinking. Sadly, this can paralyze you since your brain doesn't get the rest that it deserves. Gradually, you will notice a decrease in your productivity. You are unlikely to feel good about yourself since there is little that you achieve. Worrying too much about not being able to sleep can make you uneasy and you may find yourself in a state of captivity.

You Always Live in Fear

Are you afraid of what the future has in store for you? If you answer yes to this question, then chances are that you're caged in your mind. Living in fear could drive you to resort to drugs and alcohol as your best remedy. You will gain the perception that by taking drugs, it will help you drown your sorrows and help you forget.

You're Always Fatigued

Do you always wake up in the morning feeling tired? This could be a result of stress or depression. Instead of living a productive life, you find yourself waking up late, tired, and unmotivated. This happens because you don't give your mind an opportunity to rest.

You Don't Live in the Present

Do you find it difficult to enjoy life? Why do you think you find it daunting to sit back, relax, and be happy with your friends? The mere fact that you can't stay in the present implies that you won't focus on what is happening in the present. Overthinking blinds you from noticing anything good that is currently happening around you. You will often think about the worst that can happen. The issue is that you are trapped in your mind and there is nothing outside your thoughts that you can constructively think about.

You crave for affection, yet don't always get it

Often, overthinking is just a ploy to get attention. While this isn't always the case, it might be worth asking yourself if it is just the comfort that you seek.

You pay attention to others' assessments as well

Considering the opinions of others is crucial in understanding your feelings and what you can do about those issues which worry you.

An overthinker attempts to locate importance in all things

Indeed, everything is urgent, everything is a life and death struggle, and everything is headed toward a tragic end.

Experience the ill effects of sleep deprivation

It is common for overthinkers to lose sleep regularly. While it's normal when you have something important to worry about, the chronic overthinker will experience sleep deprivation issues as a result of their pathological worrying.

Overthinkers recollect every word and detail from a discussion

If you find yourself keeping a play by play account of your conversations, then there is a very good chance you fall under the category of overthinkers.

Overthinkers have trouble relating to others

These folks will find it hard to build lasting relationships especially if they are bent in seeing the worst of every situation.

When your mood constantly changes

Overthinking causes hormonal imbalance in people, which is manifested by frequently occurring mood swings. Also, a person may experience anxiety, obsessive-compulsive disorder, addictions, and other mental health issues.

When you notice weight variations

Overthinking causes stress, which leads to weight variations. It causes loss of appetite and loss of weight. Weight loss can happen over a few days, weeks, or even a few months. That is how the body responds to overthinking habits that increase metabolism. The body uses 'fuel' from the body's fat reserves when metabolism increases. In that way, a person experiences weight loss.

When you are anxious and restless

Too much thinking leads to anxiety and restlessness, which, if not treated, become worse over time. When a person constantly thinks about finding a job, or feeling nervous before doing a big exam, or being embarrassed in particular social situations, her mind becomes restless, and even causes the person to develop fear.

When you lack patience

A person will often feel impatient when they become too much engrossed in their thoughts. They may also become angry, irritated, and intolerant.

The body reacts to overthinking by releasing adrenaline or cortisol, which helps the body to respond to a stressful situation. For overthinkers, a stressful situation could be as small as someone else interrupting their thoughts. The overthinker will react in a way that could irritate another person.

Chapter 11 Decluttering Your Thoughts, Your Life Obligations, Your Relationships and Your Surroundings

Decluttering Your Thoughts

We all worry from time to time. You worry about yourself and others on a daily basis. This is normal, to an extent. You may worry about the potential of failure, about your safety, or other possible factors. It is instinctual, as animals must worry about their hunger until they feed themselves. However, there is a certain point where worrying is unhealthy. If you find yourself constantly worrying to the extent where it takes over your life, you need to take action. You must be able to enjoy your life. While you will certainly worry occasionally, it should not prevent you from completing your daily tasks. When worrying becomes severe, it needs attention.

You must learn to stop worrying. There is always the chance of a negative event occurring, but you must be able to find positivity and hope instead of dwelling on the potential for something going wrong. You must be able to live in the moment and focus on enjoying yourself instead of worrying about what you did incorrectly in the past and what could go wrong in the future. Here are some ways on how to declutter your thoughts:

Stop Worrying

It sounds simple enough: just stop worrying. Although this seems easier said than done, it is possible to train your brain to worry less and be able to enjoy yourself more. Worrying can be lessened, and you may greatly minimize it and even prevent it from occurring. However, this will take a lot of practice and patience with your progress. If you tend to worry naturally, this will be an ingrained habit that will take time to replace with better habits. You must be able to change your mind so that you may reduce the amount of worrying that you do.

Live in the Moment

Learning to live in the moment can really help you to stop worrying. Often, worrying is a result of the past or future. We don't typically worry as much about what we are doing in the present. You must be willing to accept the past and live without regrets. Every mistake is a learning opportunity, and every issue will only make you stronger. The future is unpredictable; the best you can do is to work your hardest towards making it a future you want. However, that's pretty difficult when you spend your time worrying!

Stop the "What-Ifs"

Everyone experiences "what-if" thoughts from time to time. This is normal and can help with the decision-making process. However, they can harm your daily life when they start to interfere with your routine. If you struggle to go about your everyday routine because you are too focused on the potential for negativity, you need to make changes to yourself regarding your worrying. When you can't control your thoughts, it's problematic.

To control these thoughts, you can try a few methods. One way is to write down these thoughts when they occur. By doing so, you are becoming more informed of how you think, and you may realize that these thoughts lack logic behind them. It will help you to realize what you are thinking, and you may understand why you think that way as a result. You should also take action on these thoughts. If there is a way to solve the problem that you are worried about, do it. If there isn't, find a way to let go of that thought. Talk to someone, write it down, or think it through. You may also take a moment to understand what the thought is, how it makes you feel, and what your reaction to it is. This will help you to have a better emotional response to it and behave properly to solve the issue. You must also become more comfortable with change and uncertainty. Recognize that some things will simply remain unknown until they occur and worrying will not alter the outcome.

Become More Aware of Yourself

Self-awareness can really help you. It can make it much easier for you to understand your emotions and feel more in control of your mind. You will realize why you act and think the way that you do. You can understand what your strengths and weaknesses are. It will also help you realize what motivates you. You will become more aware of your purpose and goals in life.

To become more self-aware, you will have to make a conscious effort to do so at first. Take some time each day to really reflect on how you are feeling. Understand your current emotions, the causes of them, and the effect they have on you. You may also reflect on your day as a whole. Did you accomplish what you set out to do? If not, what held you back from doing so? Use this time to constructively criticize yourself. Do not simply criticize yourself, compare yourself to others, or think about how you failed. Instead, realize what worked for you and what did not. Doing so will benefit you, as you can learn from that and apply it to the next day. You will not be perfect at first, but if you can make improvements each day, you will be much better off. Only compare yourself to who you were yesterday. You should always be learning, improving, and changing for the better. This is a natural way to progress in life, and it's important to do so to be the best person that you possibly can be. Remember to think about both what can be improved and what you did well, as it is important to remind yourself of your successes and remember that you are capable of success.

You may ask others to help you in several ways. One way is to talk out your emotions with another that you trust. This can help you to verbally express your thoughts. You may also ask others for feedback, as they will be able to give you an opinion outside of yourself. However, this must be healthy. You should trust the other person's word and ensure that you take everything they say as a way to improve, not as an attack on the person that you are.

It's important to stop your habit of worrying, and there are a few ways that you can work on it. You must, however, keep in mind that it will take work to stop yourself from worrying. It's also important to discover how to live in the moment so that you can enjoy life and feel greater happiness. Stopping the "what-ifs" that you think can really help you. Most of these are unnecessary, and you will feel better for not thinking these thoughts. Finally, you must become more aware of yourself to worry less.

Decluttering Your Relationships

The first step to breaking out of any toxic relationship is to identify the signs around you, acknowledge and then accept them as a truth that is negative to your health and needs to be amended. Everyone's relationships are different, but here is a closer look at some of the most common signs connection to toxic relationships:

- Emotional manipulation is one sign that is prominent in any kind of toxic relationship or connection

- The definition of this symptom varies because it can include a wide range of actions and behaviors that vary from case to case

- At its core though, emotional manipulation refers to the intentional alteration of behaviors or way of speaking in order to avoid or manage the emotions of someone else

- In the case of the toxic person, this can refer to an intentional intensification of tense emotions and responses when their friend or partner is talking in order to get them to leave the room or feel powerless in their current situation

- In the case of the victim, they know that when their friend or partner is in this mood that their tense emotions will only intensify if they try to talk to them so instead they intentionally find something to do in a different room to avoid talking to their friend or partner until they are in a better headspace

- Isolating oneself from other close connections with family or friends to spend more time with their toxic friend or partner

- In many cases, this isolation is directly linked to and even the result of their friends and family seeing the way their loved one has changed in this relationship or connection and confronted them about it

- This confrontation is seen as an act of aggression by the individual and they get defensive, siding with their toxic friend or partner and hindering their relationship with their supportive loved one

- Being dismissed as overly emotional or overreacting to things whenever you voice your feelings or opinions (particularly if they are counter to the toxic friend or partner)

- In some cases, the individual is not dismissed but rather teased and ridiculed making them feel even worse about speaking their mind

- They can be accused of imaging problems that do not exist if there is an issue the toxic friend or partner does not want to deal with

- Some toxic partners might try to make the individual feel selfish or guilty if their thoughts, opinions or desires are centered around anything they need or want

- A variety of controlling behaviors have been associated with toxic relationships and connections

- Calling a person names and speaking with a sarcastic tone in situations where it is inappropriate or hurtful

- Endless and harmful criticism that is meant to damage their self-esteem and confidence so that they are easier to control and manipulate

- Using intimidation and fear tactics when the person becomes too bold or exploratory for their liking

- Blaming the person from things they had no control over or were not even connected to and throwing out unnecessary accusations in an attempt to make their partner feel guilty about something that may not even have happened

Whatever the specifics are with toxic people, they are unhealthy influences on men and women of any age or profession. The more toxic people that are around and the longer or more connected their relationship with the individual becomes, the more power and negative influence they will have on the person. These types of relationships are often neglectful and even dangerous, and they can be some of the most difficult to break free from.

Decluttering Your Surroundings

1. Determine the department of the house you want to start decluttering.

This is the first and foremost step you need to undertake. You can't declutter all the areas of the house in a day. Even you do, that means you, leaving work, school or that vital task that you were supposed to handle for the day. It can be so overwhelming if you think you can declutter your home in a day, especially if it's your first time. It can also be time consuming, so you need to decide where you are going to start decluttering from. Start with the easiest one so that you won't get tired easily. Then, ascend to harder areas. When you have chosen an area to declutter, it's time to move to the next step on this list.

2. Give yourself 5-10 minutes decluttering period.

Decluttering is a gradual process. A process that you ought not to rush. You can dedicate 5 or 10 minutes of your time every day to declutter your home. As you proceed, increase the time and add more tasks on your list as you go on. For example, the first day can be 5 minutes. The second can be 10, the third can be 15, and so on. Don't start decluttering with 10 minutes on your first day and spend 5 minutes the next day. It simply won't work. Before you realize, you are finding it hard to dedicate even a minute to declutter your home. Start with the lowest possible time and ascend accordingly.

3. Get a trash bag ready

You would want to get rid of those items that are causing your home to be cluttered. Get a trash bag, throw them inside. Old items that you feel you don't want to get rid of, give them to charity. If you're going to store any item, get large boxes. Move them to the appropriate places and create space in your home. You will be amazed to see the number of trash bags that you have taken away.

4. Create a to-do list of items you want to throw in the trash

Surely, there will be a good number of items in trash bags that you would want to get rid of. Get a paper, write out all the items that you want to get rid of. Each item that you take to the trash cross them on your list. Also, it's important you create a to-do list of all your tasks, so that you cross each one you have accomplished. As you get rid of each item, the clutters get reduced. Creating these lists will help you keep track of tasks that you have completed and the ones that you haven't. It's easier to declutter if you have a picture of where and how to get started.

5. Declutter one item every day.

Each day that you decide to declutter your home, try to at least get an unwanted item out of your home. Imagine doing this for a month? That's 30 items. Do this for a year, and you must have for rid of 365 items. How about you increase it to 2 items every day? In no time, you will be able to declutter your house and get those items thrown into the trash. Your home will stay completely clean and devoid of dirt.

6. Take a picture

This isn't necessary, but it's quite helpful. You can decide to take a picture of a cluttered area, like your kitchen and then, take another picture of your kitchen. This time, a decluttered one. Observe those photos, and you will see how proud you have become that you have begun the step in decluttering your home.

7. Use the four-box system

Establishing a system will make it easier to declutter your home than having none. The four-box system is an example of such systems that will help you become more efficient in tidying up your home. Get four boxes and label them as follows with descriptions.

- Give away: These are boxes that should be filled with things that you don't need or use but are still okay. In other words, these are items that you can either sell online or donate to some charity organizations.

- Keep: These boxes should contain items that you plan on keeping. They are items that you can't do without. That is the items that you use frequently. Examples of these items are your clothes, sound system, chairs, etc. They mostly have a fixed place where they are kept.

- Return: In this box, things that are misplaced in your house should be kept in this box. For example, your soap shouldn't be in the sitting room. Your cutlery shouldn't be in the bathroom, and so on. These items should be kept in their appropriate places and not the other way round.

- Trash: Items or possessions that are worthless should be kept in this box.

Each room that you enter identify items that should be placed in their respective boxes. Any item at all, irrespective of its size, should enter their appropriate boxes. It may take you some time, but it's worth it. You will discover items and will now what to do with them.

8. Don't be afraid to ask for assistance

Asking for help from a friend or relative is a cool way to get suggestions on how to declutter your home. Your friend or relative can go through all the items in your home and suggest which one is to be thrown, given out, or which one is to be kept. You might want to defend your reasons for keeping such an item, which is totally cool. If your friend or relative see the same reasons as you do, then your decision is valid. If otherwise, then it's wise to get rid of such item.

The best thing about this is that your friend or relative doesn't need to be a professional to help you get rid of any clutter. Just that having someone by your side all through the decluttering process will make it easier and faster for you to get rid of certain items that you have doubts getting rid of.

Chapter 12 Mental Declutter Habits

Mental clutter can greatly lower your productivity because you will lose focus and concentration. Assess your life, identify the source of your mental clutter, and try to fix it. Remember the design of the brain does not allow it to divide its attention in too many directions. That is the reason why it needs to be orderly and peaceful so that it can filter information into the right place and act.

To get your mind in a good state, you need to clear it of any clutter. You should organize your thoughts, worries, and tasks so that your mind can have somewhere for focusing and acting accordingly. The following are some of the tips that can help you to get rid of mental clutter.

1. Declutter Your Physical Environment.

When you sit in an environment that is full of clutter, it will cause your mental clutter. This is because the clutter will keep on telling your mind that it needs to work extra hard to clear the clutter. These excessive stimuli will likely suck your mental energy. If you clear the clutter from your physical environment, you will also be clearing your mind from the mental clutter.

Get rid of the non-essential items and put everything else in its rightful place. The best way to clear your mental clutter is by clearing your environment or workspace every day so that clutter does not pile up. Tidying up your workspace will promote your mental clarity.

2. Write a "to-do" list

You do not have to overwork your brain by storing so much information in it. Having a "to-do" list where you write all that you have to do will free up your mind. The list should have priorities of tasks and you should check them daily and work on them depending on their priorities on the list. The list can have appointments, projects, bills to pay and so on. You can always tick against a task when you complete it.

3. Keep a journal

A journal is almost similar to a "to-do" list but here you document those things that disturb your peace of mind and give you anxieties and worries. You can write down your worries, plans for achieving certain goals, and even problems in your relationship that are draining your peace of mind.

4. Commit to remain in the present

You need to let go of your past. Holding on to regrets from past mistakes or missed opportunities, or people who have hurt you, will clutter your mind and rob you of your mental peace. Getting rid of unnecessary thoughts and fears will reduce stress and improve your confidence. These negative memories do not help you at all so try to delete them in your mind so that you can have a better focus on the things that are more important in your life.

5. Avoid multitasking

Organize your work well and tackle them on a priority basis. This will prevent you from straining and you will reduce stress and overwhelm. Multitasking will eventually limit your concentration span and stress you. If you find your home or office is in a mess, start by clearing the clutter before handling any other business. Clear your mind of any other thoughts and focus on clearing the clutter.

6. Limit the amount of information you consume

The amount of information that we consume can have an impact on our mental health. Too much information from the media, newspapers and the internet can clog our brain causing stress and anxiety. Spending so many hours reading some information on social media, blogs or any other platform can clutter our minds with unnecessary stuff causing mental fatigue and mental stress.

You should limit the amount of time on social media and select only important information to read. You should never allow yourself to consume negative content and cancel any blog subscription that does not help improve your life. Ensure that the information you read is authentic and from a credible source, then store only relevant information while you discard the rest.

7. Set priorities

What are your goals in life? You should identify which things are most important in your life and which ones are not. Setting priorities can help you in taking control of your life and it can help you in identifying and reaching your goals in life. Having an endless "to-do" list can clutter your mind. You should know that you could not do everything in one go. So, decongest your mind by having a top priorities list.

You can start by writing down a list of what you want to do and achieve based on priorities. The next thing is to plan on how you will do the tasks and how you will achieve your goals. After writing down how you are going to execute your plan, you can now allocate each task the time you will take to finish it. Keep checking and updating your priorities to ensure that they remain relevant because they can change over time.

8. Make decisions on time

Postponing decision making will clutter your mind with pending decisions. So, act right away and avoid procrastination. However, remember to evaluate your decisions first before implementing them. Therefore, if you delay decisions, you are simply cluttering your mind. Check your emails, letters, bills, requests and respond to them accordingly so that they do not pile up giving you mental clutter.

9. Practice meditation

Meditation is a great way of relaxing your mind and clearing it of any stressful thoughts. You need to make it a daily practice to help you eliminate any unnecessary thoughts and to calm your mind.

10. Take some time to unwind

Take a break from your busy schedules and stressful situations. Take a walk in the park, go swimming, go to social events, and go for hikes or anything that will calm you and make you happy. Give your mind rest and let it recharge so that you can improve your focus and mental clarity.

11. Share your thoughts

Sometimes talking to someone eases the emotional burden and clutter in our minds. You can share your thoughts with a trusted friend or a family member. This can help you to see things differently and make sound decisions.

12. Practice breathing exercises

Taking a deep breath and exhaling slowly can work magic by calming your mind and relaxing your nerves. Deep breathing can also clear your mind giving you a calm mood. It is also helpful in reducing stress and promoting concentration.

13. Eat healthily and get enough sleep

A good diet and good sleep are essential to your mental health. Getting enough sleep will help your mind to rest and recharge. This is also the best remedy for reducing stress and fighting depression and anxiety.

Chapter 13 What Should You Know About Hypnosis?

Hypnosis is a different, stronger form of meditation. It is something that needs more guidance as you progress. With this practice, we will provide you with commands that help reshape your brain. Let your mind wander and keep it open so we can provide you with the right kind of tools to tweak the way you think ever so slightly.

You need to be completely relaxed in order to be properly hypnotized. We are going to start this hypnosis first by making sure that you are regulating your breathing and that you are free from any tension. Once you have found that relaxed state of mind, it will be easier for our guided hypnosis to tap into the deepest parts of your brain. Make sure that you are willing to let your thoughts go and don't stay too attached to any negative emotions that pass through your mind in this process.

These thoughts and commandments will make it easier for you to keep a positive outlook each and every day. Towards the end, if you stick with it, you will be astonished at the vast improvement to your overall mental health.

Hypnosis for Life-Changing Positive Thinking

In this hypnosis, what you're going to do first is to make sure you are in a very comfortable seated position where your legs and your arms are loose. You don't want to keep anything bent to the point where you might cut off circulation. Position yourself in a way that blood can flow easily through your body.

These are going to help you better create a positive mindset rather than trying to do this all on your own. We are going to be giving you what you need to understand. These are your daily thoughts, and things that you are going to constantly need to remind yourself. We will use these thoughts to rewire your brain.

Begin by noticing your breath. Notice it come in and out, in and out. It is a very natural process that is making you feel so much better from the moment you begin.

The air needs to cycle through your body because it is what's helping you get stronger and grow into a healthier person. It keeps your blood regulated, which is very important for feeling good. When your mind feels good, your body is going to feel good, and that will show. Keep your eyes open for just a moment. Right now, look up as high as you possibly can. Do not move your head. Only look using your eyes. Look up so high that you can see your eyelids. On three, you're going to snap forward and look straight ahead of you. Then we're going to close your eyes and countdown, so first begin by looking up. Look up as high as you can. You should only see your eyelids and nothing else. Do not move your head. On the count of three, you're going to snap and then look straight ahead.

One, two, three.

Now, place your head gently back onto a pillow or something else where you can rest it comfortably for the next several minutes.

Begin by breathing in, once again. Breathe in as we count down from five. Breathe out as we count up from five. Counting down is going to get you prepared and counting up is going to help build that energy so that this hypnosis is a lot easier. Breathe in for five, four, three, two, and one. Breathe out for one, two, three, four, and five. And again. Breathe in for five, four, three, two, and one. Breathe out for one, two, three, four, and five.

You should now be incredibly relaxed and focused. It is time to make a promise to yourself. This hypnosis is going to be like a contract that you are signing with yourself, to think more positively. By the end, you should have a new, healthier mindset that will take away the mental blocks and make it easier for you to get the things that you want from life. No longer will you have to live with mental anguish, constant anxiety, or depression that only makes it harder for you to find happiness.

You are doing something good here. You are doing something healthy.

Staying positive is never a bad thing. Being positive is good. It is going to help you achieve the things that you want the most.

The first promise that you are going to make to yourself is to always look for the positives. You are going to do whatever you can to make sure that you see the bright side. Your mind is going to have to learn how to be able to pick up on a different perspective.

No matter what happens in life, you will now be an expert at finding the good. Even in situations that are difficult with no silver lining, you will know exactly what you need to do in order to find the positive side. You will be able to recognize the good from the bad.

This does not mean that you will lose your grasp on the reality of the situation. There are plenty of bad situations that you have to deal with. Each one with varying degrees of severity. Knowing how to find the positives doesn't mean that you are ignoring it.

You are now somebody who is focused on making sure that the positives are more apparent. We don't want to overlook the positive, just like how we might overlook the negative. You are going to be able to pick up on both sides of the coin. You will realize the black and the white while understanding that the gray still exists.

No matter how small this distinction might be or how fine the line is, you will understand the truth.

Let's do another breathing exercise now to make sure that this sticks in your mind. Repeat this, as a promise to yourself.

Say now, "I will always look for positivity."

To establish this further, let's breathe in again. Breathe in now for five, four, three, two, one, and breath out for one, two, three, four, and five.

Repeat, "I will always look for positivity."

Breathe in now for five, four, three, two, one, and breathe out for one, two, three, four, and five.

Now let's move on to the next commandment. You are always going to accept the things that are out of your control.

A positive life does not mean one where we will never have to deal with negative issues again. We are always going to run into things that are beyond our control. Now, at this moment, completely relaxed, happy, open, and free, you are also accepting of all things.

You are going to know exactly what to do in a situation where you don't have all of the power.

It is not always going to be that easy, but when you are dedicated and passionate, you can make sure to keep a positive mindset.

When you are presented with a challenging situation, you will be able to identify if you have any control over it or not. You will be able to understand whether there is something that you can change, or if things are just the way they are for a reason.

You are always going to look for a way to find positivity, but when you cannot, you will focus instead on making sure that you at least have a good mindset. When you are continuously focused on the negative and not looking for ways to make it a positive experience, that is only going to hold you back.

You have to realize that it is going to be a struggle, and there will still be challenges. You are promising to yourself that you are going to accept the things that are out of your control. You are okay with this because you know that in the end, it is going to make you a stronger person.

You know you can't control other people. You are aware that there will always be a certain level of uncertainty, even in the most planned out situations. You understand that even when we have a specific outcome in mind, things still won't end up looking exactly the same as we might have predicted. You accept the fact that you will not always be able to change these situations. You are very aware of things that you control and the things that you cannot. You are going to use a positive mindset to help you work through the issues that you have.

This is a promise that you're going to make to yourself.

Continue to focus on your breathing. Notice the way that the air is coming in and the way that it is leaving your body. This is to help keep you relaxed and let these thoughts come into your mind as if you were creating them on your own.

Breathe in now for five, four, three, two, one, and breath out for one, two, three, four, and five. You promise to accept the things that are out of your control.

Repeat this phrase: "I will accept the things that are out of my control."

Breathe in now for five, four, three, two, one, and breathe out for one, two, three, four, and five.

Repeat one more time. "I accept the things that are out of my control."

The next commandment is that you are always going to look for ways to include more positive activities into your life. There are many things that we can do, aside from having a healthy mindset to increase overall positivity. This includes things like eating healthy, exercising, getting the proper amount of sleep, and hanging out with people that we love. Also doing artistic activities, mindfulness activities, puzzles, and other fun solitary games will increase your ability to focus.

You are always going to look for things that make you feel good. It doesn't have to be one of these activities. These are just some common things that people enjoy helping make themselves feel good. You are promising yourself now that you will find something that makes you happy.

Pick out an activity that you can do when you are extremely stressed. Find something that will always put you in a better mood. You are going to be looking for something to increase your overall good feelings. You will be able to better decipher the difference between something that makes you feel good and something that you just simply feel obligated to do.

You don't have to subject yourself to tasks that you don't actually enjoy. There will always be certain things that we have to do, like chores or going to work, but you will know how to keep a positive mindset throughout these situations. You are always going to be looking for ways that you can include more positive activities in life. You are dedicated to yourself, to make sure that you are spending time alone and growing your skills that you enjoy more than anything else.

Breathe in now for five, four, three, two, one, and breath out for one, two, three, four, and five.

Repeat after this phrase, "I am going to look for ways to include positive activities in my life."

You are dedicated to making this promise to yourself because you want to live a happier and healthier lifestyle. You no longer want to live in misery, where you don't feel like you have an identity, or where you can find joy from simple things that you used to do.

Repeat the phrase for is one more time. "I am always going to look for ways to include more positive activities into my life."

Breathe in now for five, four, three, two, one, and breath out for one, two, three, four, and five.

Moving on to the fourth commandment. You will allow yourself some discomfort from time to time. Don't try to avoid these uncomfortable moments, whether it is stress from work or a relationship issue, you have accepted that life will always have its flaws.

There will always be moments that you wish that you didn't have to go through. This might include significant change or loss. These are natural things in life that should not be ignored. We cannot pretend as though we are free from ever having to experience a bad situation. There will always be challenges that you have to learn how to overcome.

The best way to overcome these things is through the use of your positive mindset. You are going to be able to work through these challenges because you are thinking positively. You are going to be able to pull yourself from even the most challenging situations because you understand what it takes to live happier and healthier. You are aware of all the ways that a positive mindset is going to help you work through some of these most challenging issues.

You are going to keep the endpoint in focus and not just the bright side. You now know that you are stronger and better because of these issues, especially in the aftermath. You are promising to yourself that you won't avoid these situations. You are not somebody who pretends everything is fine. You are going to confront the issues head on.

You will come face to face with your biggest fears and your greatest struggles. You will know exactly what it takes to get through the most challenging situations. You are going to be incredibly understanding that there will always be moments in life that we wish didn't happen. You are going to know exactly how to get through these. You are going to do everything within your power to make sure that you are living a healthier life in the long run.

Breathe in now for five, four, three, two, one, and breath out for one, two, three, four, and five. Repeat this statement. "I am going to allow myself to feel discomfort in order to learn."

This does not mean that you will be intentionally torturing yourself. This also does not mean that you are living in constant misery. It simply means that you aren't going to run from fear. You will not run from the hard situations.

The fifth and final commandment is always knowing how to identify a positive. Being able to see the good and pull it out is a skill that you'll need to develop. At first, you're going to be stuck on the negative, and that keeps you thinking everything is always bad.

Rather than continuing on with that mindset, you promise yourself that you are going to be like an investigator in life. You will always be able to pick up on all the clues that lead to something being more positive. It will be a lot easier for you to know exactly what is good and bad in your life.

Breathe in now for five, four, three, two, one, and breath out for one, two, three, four, and five.

You are going to continually remind yourself that you have everything that it takes to live a happier and healthier life. You will always know how to find the positive even the most challenging negative situations. Repeat after this.

"I promise to always know how to identify the positive in everything that comes my way."

Breathe in now for five, four, three, two, one, and breath out for one, two, three, four, and five. Repeat, "I am always going to know how to identify the positive and everything that comes my way."

You are going to make sure that you are doing everything possible to live a happy and healthy life. You are somebody who is ready to come face to face with the challenging things that you struggle with. You know exactly what it takes to live a happy life. You won't be waiting around for somebody else to tell you what to do anymore. You take action and live the life that you choose.

You are always going to be looking for ways that you can find positivity and even the darkest of times. You are resourceful, and this means using everything that comes your way and recovering value from it, you are exceptionally skilled, talented, and knows what they have to do to get the things that they want. You are somebody who is always going to be looking for ways that you can increase your experiences.

You take value in even the smallest most minuscule moments, and you know exactly what to do in order to make sure that you are living a happier and healthier life. You are not afraid of anything that is going to come your way. You are prepared and ready for all that you will have to face. You are in control of your life.

You are focused on your breathing once again. You feel so grateful for all the air that is coming in and leaving your body. You know everything to find the positive, even in the most negative situations, you are prepared, relaxed. You are calm, you are collected, and you are cool. You are perfectly happy. You are positive, and you are prepared. You are resourceful, and you are virtuous. You will always be looking for the good and all that you see.

As we countdown for 20, continue to focus on this.

Once we reach one, you will be snapped out of hypnosis. You will be able to continue with your life, always living by these commandments that we have wired into your psyche.

Chapter 14 Managing Stress and Anxiety with Relaxation Techniques

Many people within society are facing severe issues about anxiety. Some people end up losing their lives while a good number leads to a frustrating experience for the rest of their lives. Emotionally, they are failing on how to control themselves. Usually, anxiety forms part and parcel of our emotions. Sometimes, it is healthy and falling on the positive side of your health. In this case, you may call it a good feeling. However, anxiety can build up in a person to some toxic level. You end up harboring anxiety at a disproportionate level, forcing you to make a short call at the hospital. That is a situation of a medical disorder. Your mental health starts incurring diagnoses that result in severe fear, worry, excessive nervousness, and even apprehension.

Disorders have high impacts on the behavior of someone. Your mind gets altered, and all these lead to physical symptoms, which are very severe and sometimes harsh. You start experiencing some strange emotions. Therefore, you can either have mild anxiety or severe anxiety. In the case of severe anxiety, you will emotionally suffer, and this will affect your day to day activities. However, mild anxiety has got vagueness issues plus unsettling kind of disturbances. Therefore, due to what has been so far, we can now define anxiety. Anxiety refers to an emotion embraced with wild thoughts, tension, feelings, and even physical changes such as high impulse rates. You can control and manage your anxiety in many ways, such as meeting your demands. Doing the correct thing and filling those gaps that caused you this kind of stress will help you a lot. However, you can also control the level of your anxiety through a proper step by step meditation. We are going to take a look at the meditation techniques you can employ or implement to counter your anxiety.

The first meditation technique in this category is breathing. When you are emotionally anxious, your impulse increases, leading to faster breathing. You may feel droplets of sweat at your armpits and face. You will feel lightheaded and sometimes wholly dizzy. At this moment, getting your breath at a stable level becomes a little bit difficult. There are several meditation techniques you can do to overcome the anxiety and bring your breathing under management. These include the following:

You can start by sitting in a comfortable place and completely quiet. Place your hand on the stomach and the other hand on your chest. Breathe in and out, slowly making sure your stomach moving faster than the chest.

Next, use your nose to have regular and slow breathing in and slowly breathe out using your mouth. Try as much as possible to watch your hands, sensing them more often. Your hand at the chest should not move; however, you should slightly move the other side across the stomach.

Now your anxiety is a little bit becoming weak. You can go ahead with this process as many times as you wish till you feel a little bit relaxed. At this moment, your anxiety will lessen up.

Secondly, visualize. In this case, you can work on your visualization state of mind. It will help you realize a happy place in your mind. Visualization paints a flowering picture in your mental mind. It comes a feeling of relaxation, and this will eventually calm and cool both of your body and brain. You are anxious, look for a comfortable place, and remain completely quiet and silent. Start having thoughts of your best site for relaxing. While you are doing this, try to think of a place that gives you peace, happiness, and more so, a calming state of mind. However, this place can be either in the real world or instead of a hypothetical situation. You should put more effort here to get the optimum level of relaxation. More so, this place should also be more comfortable to think about and use it as a future referral to all of your anxiety conditions.

Now go ahead with your visualization. Take your time to think of those small details and things you would find in that place if at all you were there. Think of the feeling of the site, how it would smell and sound. In sound, I mean all kinds of music within the happy atmosphere, and this would be caused by the following factors such as birds, swaying of trees, and so on. Think of the rivers flowing with a soothing sound and a cooling effect of wind breeze. Start envisioning yourself while thoroughly enjoying and making fun in that place. Now that you have this picture in your mind, you can start by closing your eyes and making some regular but slow breathes using your nose and breathing out through your mouth. Maintain both the breathing and visualization process until your anxiety starts to lessen. Since your anxious emotion will lift, do not forget to revisit this place during anxiety conditions.

You can also do exercises that relax your muscles, whether within the short run or long run. Anxiety causes tension, strain, exhaustion, and weakness of your muscles. In most cases, it is not that much; however, sometimes, this cannot allow you to concentrate on other issues. Muscle stress act as a hindrance to your anxiety management. It has that nagging and annoying trend of creating difficulty in your way to control your anxiety. Therefore, the only way to achieve your anxiety elimination is to first destroy or eradicate any element of stress within your muscles. There are several meditation exercises that you can get on your way to start the process, as you can see below. Since you want to delete muscle tension during anxiety moments, you can do the following:

☐   Look for the right comfortable place and in total silence. Make sure you have closed your eyes and concentrate on your breathing. Breathe in and out for sometimes. Make sure it is slow breathing, which you do with your nose and breathe out using your mouth.

☐   Still breathing, make a tight fist using your hand and tightly squeeze your fist.

☐   While still squeezing your fist, hold it for few seconds and detect all the strain and tension you are feeling now, especially in your hand.

☐   Go ahead by opening your fist, note how you feel in this situation. At this juncture, you may notice some element of tension deserting you, and this reflects on your hand, resulting in a more relaxed and lighter situation.

Another meditation technique you can also employ to counter anxiety is counting. Many people always avoid it for various reasons that are funnily unknown to me even though several books of psychology talk much about it. Many psychologists, taking psychological therapy as a living or as a hobby, also are busy doing it to their clients. Counting is a simple and easy way to ease up your anxious mind. When you get yourself in that mix of anxiety, get yourself the right place; make sure it is a little bit quiet and silent. It should be comfortable too since that will create a relaxing feeling without many disturbances. After meeting up with these conditions, you can go ahead with your counting process. Start counting from one to ten, and you can go with this even up to 20 times. Counting is not limited; therefore, you can move to higher figures until you feel you are recuperating well. That is, your anxiety is lifting and subsidizing tremendously. Sometimes, you might get a quicker and faster relief; however, other times, this may prove to take a little bit longer. In this case, you should only be patient and stay calm as you focus on your emotional healing process. It is better to note that healing is a process that requires patience and time.

Staying present is also another meditation technique that will help you counter your level of anxiety. You must look for ways to create your mindfulness at all times. That's, you should practice as hard as possible to be present in your state of mind, and no one should judge you under any circumstances. Staying in this situation will help you eradicate several groups of anxiety that might be building up. Therefore, you can at least bring back your state of mind by doing the following exercises:

☐ Look for a quiet place and make sure it is very comfortable where you can eventually sit while closing your eyes.

☐ You can as well make a note on how you feel, especially about your body, and this should be extended to your breathing too.

☐ After this, make a slight change in your awareness of your surroundings. Take every note of anything that's happening, especially in the external world. What you smell or even here will eventually bring back your physical balance in terms of your mindfulness. Again, there is that feeling of an environment that will invade your presence. This will also give you that chance of having your present state back, thus countering your anxiety.

☐ You can also change your awareness by shifting it from your environment to your body. Repeat it until your anxious mind become free, and the level of anxiety diminishes ultimately.

You can also counter anxiety by interrupting it. That is, interrupting your thinking here. It is always hard to have an honest thought when you have a high level of stress. Again, even less level, such as mild anxiety, instills in you that unsettling feeling that prevents you from thinking very well. Anxious thinking is hazardous since you might end up thinking of something that's not true. You end up making severe accusations followed by some critical steps in life that you might regret later on as time passes. Also, you may get yourself doing things that would only worsen your already worse situation. The only way to avoid this is by breaking the anxious thoughts that are lingering on your now stressed up mind. The following guidelines will eventually help you to come up with a clear thing far off from the anxious mind.

☐ You can start asking yourself about your usual worries and if at all these worries are complicated and offer a problem to you. If your answer is yes, then you are off to the process of starting up your meditation as quick as possible.

☐ After this, you can now start your anxiety interruptions using the following steps.

☐ You can try singing any song whether you know it or not as long as you have mastered some parts of it. Again, you can speak aloud your anxieties or try shouting or talking them to yourself.

☐ After this, think of an excellent task for your next focus instead of your anxiety. Therefore, this focus could be on your spouse, children, a person you cherish, your happy place, or even some tasks that you have saved to undertake them later on during the day, such as having a meeting somewhere.

Another way to interrupt your anxiety is by investing much of your time in listening to music or even having some excellent collections of different books touching on various life chapters.

Last but not least, on this, try as hard as possible to handle yourself with much dignity and notice your feeling after every meditation practice you undertake. Note the way your anxiety diminishes.

Another meditation technique you can also use is the self-stress management. Anxiety comes as a result of the stress of not getting something or not achieving something. When you learn to eliminate stress, then you will be in a position to fight off your anxiety. Again, understanding how you can manage stress help you to strike off the possible triggers of your anxious mind. You can, therefore, manage this through proper organization of your upcoming deadlines and various pressures. Do this by compiling them correctly in a manner that you can eventually achieve them. Make sure that those daunting tasks are achievable and more manageable. Still on this, you can take some time off for your benefit. Locate for yourself some free time so that you can make even a nature stroll to release some hidden anxiety.

You can also offer yourself some relaxing techniques. These relaxing techniques provide you that kind of meditation feeling to counter your anxiety. There are several ways in which you can have a relaxing posture in your mind, and these include breathing exercises, resting, and even staying in the dark. Yoga, long baths, and even mild slow sex are part and parcel of these relaxing techniques that are part of meditation. Breathing exercises such as breathing in through your nose and taking and taking the air out through your mouth have been seen as good ways to release the toxic level of anxiety. Long baths, especially within the bathtub, can release some tensions within your strained body. You will feel a little relaxed in the end. As a result, this will lead to the eradication of anxiety. We have slow sex and romance, too, which also contributes to the reduction of anxiety level. If well maintained and managed, the issues of anxious thoughts and worries will never be an issue. Yoga helps you not only to reduce anxiety but also a reduction in weight. Due to this, you will lead a life free from health-related complications. There are several ways to carry out your yoga activities and always struggle to get the best. If you cannot find one, then you can consult your doctor or trainer. You can also rest in the dark for longer times as expected. Darkness is a quiet, silent place with little or no disturbance at all. In this place, you can even perform other meditation techniques such as breathing, counting, and so on. You can also listen to the sounds made by several animals within the atmosphere and expose your whole body to the prevailing fresh air. All these will leave you in a situation where you are not anxious and, if any, then very minimal or little.

Other forms of meditation techniques include performing some exercises to replace your negative thinking with positivity. On most occasions, anxiety comes about as a result of having some negative thoughts within your mind. You start off thinking of things that are not there, or instead of having a clear state of consciousness, you end up having a dirty mind. To start on this, you can make a good list of every bad or negative thought that lingers on your consciousness mind every day. Make a corresponding list but positive things you can eventually use to counteract the negative ones. You should make sure that these lists are manageable. There and then, establish a mental image with a notion of conquering all your fear. For example, you have worries about not completing your job today, and this has been bothering you for quite sometimes.

On the other hand, without completing your job today, you will have to forfeit the wages. The feeling of not getting paid at the end of the day gives you many worries that at the end of the day, you become highly anxious. The best positive thing to note down is how you can still have money. It seems in your worries, and money was the anxiety trigger. If you can as well get other sources of money as long as they are legit, then you will be able to avoid anxiety in this manner. This might be a short-run solution to the predicament, and next time you may think of having a long-term solution. As much as you look for an immediate solution about your worries that later on leads to anxiety, try as much as possible to get the long-term solution. A long-term solution, in this case, is to come up with a drafted plan containing a step by step guideline on how to complete that task within that located time. There are other meditation techniques such as getting involved in volunteering work within your society. Society is full of life-threatening and complications that affect their day to day activities. People are suffering from a particular illness due to negligence. Others are undergoing traumas caused by fire, death of the loved ones, and much more. Some, on the other hand, need physical and emotional encouragement to keep going. So, you can eventually chip in within this society and help them solve these life disputes that seem to devour them in the next moment of their lives. Touching someone's heart has the power to accelerate their lives once more. You can also get into their contribution lists and donate a few of the items you no longer need though still in good condition. Therefore, you will realize that your anxious mind and all the worries that came with it have reduced or even eliminated.

Chapter 15 What is Relaxation?

The art of relaxation is a state of mind. In other, you need to set your thoughts in such a way that leisure is essential. Even when you are eating, you can't just keep consuming all the time.

You need to relax and take some break that will help your mind settle and think of other things.

The minds also need to shift from one aspect to the other. In other words, if you keep doing something for long, there are chances that you will get bored and hate it. In the same way, you can't eat for more than an hour and expect that all is well. Even your jaws, let alone your teeth need to relax and prepare for another meal.

Also, if the snack is so sweet, there are chances that you can't take all the time and eat everything at a go. You need to relax and allow the process of digestions to swallow, let alone.

Several studies have been carried out to determine the effects of failing to relax while eating. It is worth noting that if you eat without allowing your gut to shallow well, there are chances that you will be choked.

There are other cases where one fails to register in the brain that one is full since they are not relaxing. In other words, if your minds do not have time to relax, there are some complications that one may develop.

For instance, people who develop the disorder of binge eating do not improve the condition in a single day.

However, it occurs gradually such that the minds fail to register that one is full. The desire to keep eating develops, and one thinks of eating rather than deducing anything else. They are the kind of people who will prefer eating at night, during the day and at any time. The art of eating in such a manner is not right as the mind does not relax.

Experience shows that the ritual of gratitude combines very well with the ritual of viewing ("spend" the day ritual), and from their combination, a single powerful ritual can be formed. In addition, both of these rituals are in harmony with specific assistive techniques, such as a warm bath. Among the more active components are walking, as well as all forms of active relaxation, such as muscle relaxation, according to the Jacobson method.

How to relax when something really bothers you? "Nothing will work out for me," "I am like a squeezed lemon" or "I have my nerves to the limit" - these are some of the expressions that accompany us during severe stress and anxiety. Sometimes we tend to get by with pills or even with visits to the doctor so that he will prescribe a "wonderful injection" from all problems. I will try to give you some recommendations on how you can make yourself a "wonderful injection" without having to take pills or going to the doctor. Learn to relax when you are overwhelmed by anxiety and stress! First, discover the Jacobson's Progressive muscle relaxation method.

In any case, first, we need to learn a little about what anxiety or sleep anxiety is in order to understand why there is no need to take medication to overcome it. When anxiety overcomes us, we feel a sense of fear, and even come to the conclusion that one day we can die from one of the attacks of severe anxiety: there is nowhere else to go. In this case, fear is a natural emotional response to an imminent threat, real or imagined, while anxiety is a preliminary reaction to a future threat (which may or may not occur).

Both of these concepts are productive in a sense because they warn us of the existence of danger and help us prepare for trouble. As they say, forewarned means armed. The problem arises at the moment when we are too long in a "state of alert" in high-intensity mode. This can lead to the so-called "anxiety attack," the symptoms of which cause a sharp deterioration in well-being, and as a result, we are forced to consult a doctor. However, we must understand that anxiety is nothing more than a combination of symptoms. This is not a disease, and this condition can be controlled.

Let's get back to anxiety. In order to understand what it is, imagine that a lion is chasing you, and you try to run as fast as you can. But actually, there is no lion! "Lion" exists only in our head. That is, the cause of these symptoms of malaise was the idea of something non-existent, fictitious (for example, fear of death or the obsession to die, fear of leaving home, or fear not to survive a heart attack).

In the case of the lion, we see that the solution lies in the palm of your hand: "you just have to stop," because the lion does not really exist, and there is no real danger. This would be the only way to reduce our anxiety, stop sweating, and soothe a heart jumping out of our chest. These are the same symptoms that provoke a real fit of anxiety or even panic.

The practice of conscious meditation, some fascinating activity or hobby, etc. This is something that constantly keeps your mind busy with something. So, we move away from this idea of danger (or from any other obsession), which can be a good strategy and help us reduce the symptoms of anxiety.

I will tell you about a very effective method for learning how to relax when anxiety overcomes you: the method of progressive muscle relaxation by an American scientist and Doctor Edmund Jacobson.

Jacobson's Progressive Relaxation

What is Jacobson's progressive relaxation? This is a physiological method focused on the state of rest. It promotes deep relaxation without much effort, which allows you to set arbitrary control over the level of bodily tension. It allows you to recognize the close relationship between the level of bodily tension and mental stress, and to understand that the reduction of one of them involves the relief of the other.

It helps to achieve a state of dominance and relaxation in a gradual but continuous form (progressive relaxation), each time more intense and effective. The method teaches us to relax the muscles with the help of willpower, and through this, we achieve a deep state of inner peace, which comes when excessive bodily tension leaves us.

The areas in which stress builds up are numerous, and sometimes they cannot be seen with the naked eye, so it is important to learn how to relax all muscle groups in the body.

What Does the Method of Progressive Muscle Relaxation of Jacobson Give Us?

Using this method, you can reduce periods of general anxiety, learn how to relax muscle tension, improve sleep quality, as well as increase self-control, and achieve a high level of relaxation. The method of progressive muscle relaxation of Jacobson consists of three main stages:

1. Tension-Relaxation

We are talking about the consistent tension and relaxation of various muscle groups throughout the body. This is done in order to learn to recognize the difference between the state of muscle tension and muscle relaxation. Thanks to this, a state of complete muscle relaxation is achieved, which is gradually transmitted throughout the body. Muscle groups should be in a state of tension for several seconds (7-8) and slowly relaxed for 5-10 minutes.

2. Observation

All participating muscle groups are mentally tested to make sure they are relaxed to the maximum.

3. Relaxation of Consciousness

At this stage, you need to think about something pleasant and positive or completely free your mind from thoughts (if you know how to do it). You need to learn how to relax your mind while your whole body continues to relax. Your meditation training comes to play here.

These three phases usually last from 10 to 15 minutes each. The method should not be applied in a hurry. This method can be repeated several times a day.

About the Jacobson Method or Progressive Muscular Relaxation

We all strain and relax to move and live. Any action is a rather complex combination of muscle contractions and relaxation. Any thought can cause a similar combination of contractions and relaxation, even if we do not take active actions, and even if it seems to us that we are not moving.

A sudden sound will make us freeze and squint our eyes towards the sound source, even if we do not turn our heads in this direction. An unpleasant conversation will cause tension in the facial muscles, and even the muscles of the upper shoulder girdle, despite the fact that we carefully monitor the expression of our face and our posture. Pleasant signals from outside also affect us: we relax, facial features soften, we catch our breath.

If our life is full of events and thoughts related to stress, muscle tension will prevail and become our habitual state to such an extent that we ourselves will not notice it. However, such an overvoltage will not be completely invisible. Sooner or later, we will find it by pain in the neck, shoulders, sore muscles, headaches associated with tension, steady gloomy facial expression, and other delights of the effects of prolonged anxiety associated with stress.

The method of progressive muscle relaxation of Jacobson is among the best ways to handle your own body to reduce the effects of stress.

The long-term psychological effects of the regular practice of progressive muscle relaxation include:

- Reducing general anxiety.

- Reduced anxiety expectations associated with phobias.

- Reducing the frequency and duration of panic attacks.

- Expanding your own capabilities in frightening situations when applying the method of desensitization (graduated exposure).

- Improving concentration.

- Increased mood control.

The practice itself is that you perform a certain sequence of simple exercises. You mentally give yourself certain commands that you yourself execute. Exercise should take place daily, preferably twice a day, at a time convenient for you and in a quiet place where you can take a comfortable position and remove or loosen clothing and accessories that are restricting you. The room should have a comfortable temperature. The supine position is optimal, but not required. Estimated lesson time is 20 minutes. Do not strain muscle groups in places where you are experiencing pain without first consulting the Energy Cleaning (EC) meditation. Try to exercise without excessive perseverance, but with enviable regularity.

Chapter 16 Relaxation Techniques for Anxiety

Relaxation is an incredibly effective way of dealing with anxiety, and it applies to all groups of people. It allows the body to activate its natural response to combat stressors. Relaxation comes in many forms and depends on what works best for you. Some of the relaxation techniques that have been proven to beat back anxiety are:

- Body scan technique

- Abdominal breathing for quick relaxation

- Progressive muscle relaxation

- Mind body relaxation to decrease stress and anxiety

- Relaxing self-massage

- Focus on breathing

- Deep breathing

- Roll breathing

- Box breathing

- Progressive relaxation

- Autogenic training

- Relaxing poses

There is a common belief among many people that relaxation involves sitting idle and or doing something you enjoy, like watching a movie or sleeping. No, relaxation is a task that needs concentration and energy input. Its sole purpose is to reduce the effects of stress and anxiety. If your definition of relaxation doesn't meet this goal, then it is far from relaxation. Relaxation achieves this by putting your body to a state of deep rest and restores normalcy such as slowing the heart rate, reducing blood pressure, improve blood circulation, and, most importantly, checking stress and anxiety. Activities that involve relaxation are those that touch on the most affected organs like the heart, blood vessels, and those in the breathing system. Try things like muscular exercises, meditation, yoga, and deep breathing. Most of these exercises are a form of self-treatment, so you don't need a professional to do them. However, they are quite demanding and require a lot of discipline. If you are the type that needs to be pushed, you might consider looking for a professional therapist to help you do the exercises. The word 'professional' is key because not anybody can make you do things that make you uncomfortable, especially if you're an adult. You need someone that will be hard and a little harsh on you. Also, people have diverse systems that respond differently to changes. If one or two of these exercises don't work for you, look for one that you are comfortable doing and is compatible with your system. You don't have to kill yourself trying to make a particular technique work even you can see that it is not working. Furthermore, all these techniques have been proven to lead to the same results, which is slowing down stress and anxiety. Just don't be too lazy to give a particular technique trial and error period before giving up on it entirely. Remember, things take time; you need to give your body a chance to get used to these changes. You will get used to those exercises in no time, and they will become a habit.

There is a thin line between relaxation exercises and meditation exercises. The main difference being that relaxation exercises engage various parts of the physical body while meditation engages the brain. The similarity between them is that they both put the entire body and mind in a state of rest to relieve affected parts and organs from stress and anxiety. Both exercises are carried out in systematic steps to the end. Skipping one step will likely jeopardize the whole process. If you are not sure about these steps and the order in which they are done, it is advisable that you seek the help of a therapist who will take you through each step.

Body Scan

As you meditate, it can be helpful to do a body scan. This involves bringing attention to each part of your body. Allow your feelings to come to the surface and release them. You can complete this exercise lying down or sitting in a recliner. Focus on your breathing first. Then notice your toes. Breathe through your body and expel tension out through your toes. Focus on sensations, tension, and feelings in each part of your body and then breathe them out through that part of your body.

Conducting a body scan helps you identify areas in which you are holding tension and learn to release it. Do this as often as you feel necessary or when tension arises.

Abdominal Breathing

Slow breathing from your abdomen can help alleviate symptoms of panic by slowing your respiratory rate, reducing the constriction of your chest wall muscles, and decreasing symptoms of hyperventilation.

When you feel dizzy or disoriented during a panic attack, it is because you are breathing rapidly from your chest. After three or four minutes of slow abdominal breathing, you should notice your symptoms are reduced. In addition to breathing this way in the moment of panic, you should also practice five minutes each day to train yourself to breathe more deeply on a regular basis.

To practice deep breathing, find a comfortable position. Close your eyes. Notice your breath. Is it shallow from your chest? Are you breathing slowly or quickly?

Now inhale deeply and slowly through your nose and expand your stomach as you breathe. Put your hands on your stomach so that you can see them rise and fall. Gradually, exhale through your mouth, letting out all of the air. If you feel worse during deep breathing, take a break for about 30 minutes and then try again.

If you practice abdominal breathing regularly, it should become natural for you. You will be able to initiate it during a panic attack to cue your body to relax.

Progressive Muscle Relaxation

This is a two-step process of muscular contraction and relaxation involving various groups of muscles in the body. This exercise is important because it demonstrates how your body physically responds to stress and anxiety. Remember, this is a mental disorder that is not easy to detect, but if we incorporate physical aspects in detection, it will be much easier to know when we are experiencing anxiety. The exercise can be combined with deep breathing to yield maximum results. For you to carry out this exercise, you must be in your best form health-wise; no muscle spasms, no back pains, or recent injuries that might put unnecessary strain on the muscles. In case you have or suspect to have any of these problems, consult your doctor before starting the exercise. Here is the procedure.

Mind-Body Relaxation to Decrease Stress and Anxiety

The purpose of this mind-body relaxation meditation is to get rid of fear and anxiety. This guided meditation session will take you deep inside your mind. You will be able to get rid of your fears and anxieties. You will get a chance to face them and defeat them.

This guided meditation is very helpful in relieving stress and anxiety. It helps you in sleeping better and provide complete physical, mental, and emotional relief. You can practice it anytime you like.

Relaxing Self Massage

The objective of this meditation session is to physically release the tension from the body through self-massage and mentally release the tension through meditation. It is going to be a completely relaxing session. You can sit in any comfortable position you want. If you wish you can sit on a chair or even in the cross-legged posture.

Focused breathing

Breathing is one of the body's involuntary actions, meaning you do not really need to command your body to breath, it just happens. However, you can turn your breathing into a form of meditation just by taking notice of every breath that you take.

In focused breathing meditation, you take long, slow, deep breaths; breaths so deep that you fill your abdomen with air as well. To practice this form of meditation, you disengage your mind from all thoughts, and focus all your attention on your breathing. This is especially helpful for when you start noticing that your thoughts are starting to go out of your control.

However, this technique might not be appropriate for those who have respiratory ailments, like asthma and some heart ailments.

Deep Breathing

Throughout any day, there are bound to be things that cause your stress levels to rise slightly. There are also going to be thoughts that pop into your head and cause you to feel anxious. Our mind can be our own worst enemy, but the good news is we can take control. There are many ways that we can help ease our fears, and deep breathing is one of them!

These techniques are extremely easy to do and can be done anywhere, even at your desk or on the bus to work! If you find it hard to concentrate, you can also purchase a guided relaxation tape, or download a stress-relieving app, as these will guide you through breathing exercises until you get the hang of doing them yourself.

This is a method you can use for any type of stress or anxiety that is bothering you, and it's a great way to get rid of an issue that is upsetting you at any stage during the day.

Another essential breathing technique is ensuring that we are taking deep, full breaths. When we are even the slightest bit stressed, we start breathing shallowly. These shallow, short breaths do not give us enough oxygen and can even lead to full-blown panic attacks. To stop poor breathing, place your hand an inch or two above your stomach. Now, slowly breathe in through your nose until your stomach touches your hand. Go with our usual 5 counts inhales and hold for a few seconds before slowly exhaling out through your mouth.

When our breathing is shallow, we only fill up the top portion of our lungs with air. Placing your hand above your stomach ensures that you are breathing deeply enough where your entire lungs are filled!

Deep breathing is the foundation of many calming strategies. It can be done on its own or with other methods like meditation, tai chi yoga, etc. Deep breathing is easy because we need to breathe to remain alive, but strongly and efficiently for mental relaxation and stress reduction. Deep breathing focuses on breathing the stomach thoroughly and clean singly. It is easy to learn that you can do it anywhere, and it regulates your stress levels. Sit down with your back straight, inhale through the nose as the belly grows. Inhale as much clean air as possible into the lungs. It makes it possible to get more oxygen into the blood. Exhale the mouth as the belly drops to force as much air as possible out and close the abdominal tract. If you find it difficult to do this sitting, first try to lie down. You could put your hands on your chest and stomach to see if it's wrong.

Roll Breathing

Roll breathing causes you to grow full utilization of your lungs and to concentrate on your relaxing. You can do it in any position. Yet, while you are learning, it is ideal to lie on your back with your knees bowed.

Practice move breathing day by day for a little while until you can do it anyplace. You can utilize it as a moment unwinding apparatus whenever you need one. Some individuals get tipsy the initial couple of times they attempt move relaxing. In the event that you start to inhale excessively quick or feel woozy, slow your relaxing. Get up gradually.

Box Breathing

One of the simplest and best breath work procedures is box breathing. No, this doesn't include sitting in one of those goliath boxes you get when you move to another house, yet rather alludes to the example itself. Known to be highly effective in promoting peaceful sleep, Box breathing includes giving equivalent time to a nasal breathe in, first breath hold, nasal breathe out, and second breath hold. The rhythm and cadence of box breathing makes it relax. It urges us to concentrate on tallying the corner of each of the four "sides."

Since the inbreath and outbreath are equivalent, this method adjusts to your sensory system and help you simply settle and bring your body and mind back to the focus. Box breathing is ideal for relaxing, especially when one of its advantages include promoting sleep.

Box breathing is an extraordinary procedure for us to deal with everyday stressors as well. The system works in a wide range of stressful circumstances. Hence, it is recommended for everyone. Except children younger than 7-8 years of age, this procedure can be advantageous to anybody, particularly the individuals who need to think or reducing stress.

It is recommended to attempt to rehearse box breathing technique for 10 to 20 minutes on a daily basis, ideally simultaneously of day. On the off chance that that target appears to be unattainable, you may attempt it for a couple of minutes at whatever point you feel and stop it when you become uncomfortable. On the off chance that you practice this technique at list for 5 minutes daily you will see a huge effect in your everyday life.

Autogenic Relaxation

This means something that comes from inside you. Using this relaxation technique requires the use of your visual imagery, as well as your bodily awareness. With this technique, you repeat affirmations and words that help you to reduce muscle tension, as well as make you relax. You can imagine a peaceful setting, and then focus your mind and relax your breathing. Meditation is one such technique that uses autogenic relaxation.

Relaxing Poses

Numerous individuals state that some poses causes them rest better. These are relaxing poses that can help you to fall asleep as they help to cultivate a quiet mind if you practice it for a period of time.

By focusing on deep breathing, and by fully relaxing and releasing your body you will evoke a meditative state. These postures are very easy and can work for anyone and you can do this sequence right in your own bed.

Neck Stretches

Your neck holds a lot of tension and stress and this is a great stretch to help to let go of some of that tension. Unlike neck rolls, which are not really very safe for your neck, this stretch is chiropractor approved!

Fan Pose

Fan Pose is a relaxing forward bend that opens up your inner thighs and stretches the lower back. It helps quiet the organs and get any stagnant energy in the legs moving again. Use this pose to direct your focus inward after a long, busy, stressful day.

Chapter 17 Understanding Guided Meditation

This is all about using your senses, such as the sense of smell, sounds, taste, textures, and sights as much as possible. You form mental images of places or situations you find relaxing in your mind, and a teacher may guide you.

Guided relaxation uses several techniques that may be used separately or in combination with each other. It may last as long as ten minutes and helps reduce impulses that trigger automatic behaviors. Guided relaxation uses abdominal breathing, visualization, progressive muscle relaxation, and mindfulness.

You will learn to breathe deeply as you imagine a serene environment using guided imagery. This sort of visualization activates the imaginative and sensory faculties of your brain. Relaxation meditation may also focus on relaxing the muscles so that you may feel the difference between tense and relaxed muscles when you are responding to stimuli. Mindfulness techniques are relaxing because the mind does not cling on one particular thought. It wanders and hops from thought, emotion, sensation, etc. Mindfulness meditation is about being present in the now.

Guided meditation is whereby you listen to the soothing voice of a meditation teacher in a meditation session to help you fall asleep. Meditation instructors give you a guide throughout the entire meditation session. An instructor may ask you to inhale deeply and exhale and relax your toes or legs. However, you should also note that this is not necessary you do with a guide by a specialist, but one can perform it alone.

Let's say you are using the help of the instructor. He/she may ask you to imagine a series of relaxing images. For example, some may invite you to imagine yourself at a beautiful sandy beach and envision yourself happily seated along the water's edge as the wavelets tickle your feet.

The clouds, the mountains, and the oceans are the most commonly chosen scenes of imaginations. However, you can choose to focus on anything you want as long as it is calming. There are no rules about what one should imagine and focus on. Some people enjoy visualizing their office- brushing everything off his/her office desk and going to sleep. One only needs to pick a place he/she feels safe, and using imaginations, invite all the senses to explore it. It is simply because the brain doesn't often know the difference between what is real and what is not. For example, when you watch a horrifying movie, your adrenaline may go up, or when you start to salivate when you imagine yourself eating something.

Apart from helping with insomnia, meditation can help one to let go of negative thought patterns and emotions, giving one insight on how to deal with grief or trauma and thus encouraging healing. Therefore, meditation has a wide array of other benefits when diligently practiced.

Meditation can also help to develop compassion towards other people. Yeah, a pretty nice and wholesome way to get to sleep! Goodnight!

Gratitude meditation is a kind of meditation, whereby instead of one focusing on the breath, it requires you to concentrate on the things you are grateful for. It is one of the easiest and effective ways to fall asleep, as one never lacks anything to be grateful for. The things you are grateful for could be something small as having a nice coffee, or something big like your partner or your job. All you need here is to challenge yourself to think of the things you are grateful for in life. I am sure such things are uncountable, now you can use them to gain some sleep if you are having trouble falling asleep at night.

Deprivation of sleep can have a devastating impact on one's health and general productivity. Therefore, it is essential to put a lot of considerations in the quality of our sleep. And since sleeping has been proven to contribute to the healing process of our body, it is high time we get some good night sleep. The good news is that you don't have to take medications for you to have a night of quality sleep. All you have to do is to put into practice one of the above meditation techniques for deep sleep and enjoy yourself a pretty good sleep.

People think that their life is complete. No. Fear pops up. Have a huge event coming. Most of the cases of anxiety are unexpected. Meditation is the cheapest way to deal with stress. It is more effective than drugs. Its effects are long-lasting. When compared to drugs, it is more affordable and more effective. This therapy is very successful in treating depression and anxiety. These effects are long-term. The method is also less costly. Just after a few months into the program, some of the patients were already well. So, meditation works better than antidepressants to reduce anxiety. The world is full of chaos. Chaos can exert some stress in you. However, with a peaceful mind, we can deal with the disorder. Therefore, this is where peace in the brain is required.

The subconscious mind is generally put off balance by two major issues, the first being fear and the latter being worry or the re-living of fear in conscious moments with conscious thoughts. In order, therefore, to cleanse the soul of all forms of negative reenactments, we have chosen to push forward with what is called guided meditation on positive consciousness.

Paths of consciousness are all intertwined. As you grow older, you will begin to realize that each of these paths underpins your actions by filtering the energy with which you choose to process your life's force. As such, the best way to rebuild your bridge to relaxation is to work on a positive filter through with you can view your own self and transform your consciousness while also healing and moving forward.

Chapter 18 Importance of Guided Meditation

You are most likely here right now because you have heard amazing, life-changing aspects meditation can bring to your life. Whether you are looking to improve your mental health, performance, physical health, or better your relationship with yourself or others; meditation could be the perfect practice for you.

Unfortunately, there are many individuals who suffer from mental health issues. Whether you are dealing with anxiety, depression, or something along those lines; meditation can help place you in a better mindset when practiced on a regular basis.

1. Decrease Depression

In a study done in Belgium, four-hundred students were placed in an in-class mindfulness program to see if it could reduce their stress, anxiety, and depression. It was found that six months later, the students who practiced were less likely to develop depression-like symptoms. It was found that mindfulness meditation could potentially be just as effective as an antidepressant drug!

In another study, women who were going through a high-risk pregnancy were asked to participate in a mindfulness yoga exercise for ten weeks. After the time passed, it was found there was a significant reduction in the symptoms often caused by depression. On top of the benefit of less depression, the mothers also showed signs of having a more intense bond with their child while it was still in the womb.

Reduce Anxiety and Depression

In general, meditation may be best known for the mental health benefits of reducing the symptoms associated with anxiety and depression. It was found that through meditation, individuals who practiced meditation such as Vipassana or "Open Monitoring Meditation," were able to reduce the grey-matter density in their brains. This grey-matter is related to stress and anxiety. When individuals practice meditation, it helps create an environment where they can live moment to moment rather than getting stuck in one situation.

While practicing meditation, the positive mindset may be able to help regulate anxiety and mood disorders that are associated with panic disorders. There was one article published in the American Journal of Psychiatry based around twenty-two different patients who had panic or anxiety disorders. After three months of relaxation and meditation, twenty of the twenty-two were able to reduce the effects of their panic and anxiety.

When you are able to relax, you would be amazed at how much better your brain will be able to function. By letting go of stress, you leave room for positive thoughts in your head and will be able to make better decisions for yourself. It's a win-win situation when you can improve your mood and your performance simply from meditation.

Better Decision Making

A study done at UCLA found that for individuals who practiced meditation for a long time, had a larger amount of gyrification in the brain. This is the "folding" along the cortex, which is directly related to processing information faster. Compared to individuals who do not practice meditation, it was found that meditators were able to form memories easier, make quicker decisions, and could process information at a higher rate overall.

Improve Focus and Attention

Another study performed at the University of California suggested that through meditation, subjects are able to increase their focus on tasks, especially ones that are boring and repetitive. It was found that even after only twenty minutes of meditation practice, individuals are able to increase their cognitive skills ten times better compared to those who do not practice mindfulness.

Along the same lines, it's believed that meditation may be able to help manage those who have ADHD, or attention deficit hyperactivity disorder. There was a study performed on fifty adults who had ADHD. The group was placed through mindfulness-based cognitive therapy to see how it would affect their ADHD. In the end, it was found that these individuals were able to act with awareness while reducing both their impulsivity and hyperactivity. Overall, they were able to improve their inattention.

Relieve Pain

It has been said that it's possible that meditation could potentially relieve pain better when compared to morphine. This may be possible due to the fact that pain is subjective. There was a study done on thirteen Zen masters compared to thirteen non-practitioners. These individuals were exposed to painful heat whilst having their brain activity watched. The Zen masters reported less pain, and the neurological output reported less pain as well. This goes to show that pain truly is a mental aspect.

Along the same lines, mindfulness training could also help patients who have been diagnosed with Fibromyalgia. In one study, there were eleven patients who went through eight weeks of training for mindfulness. At the end of the study, the overall health of these individuals improved and reported more good days than bad.

Avoid Multitasking Too Often

While multitasking can seem like a good skill to have at some points, it's also an excellent way to become overwhelmed and stressed out. Unfortunately, multitasking can be very dangerous to your productivity. When you ask your brain to switch gears between activities, this often can produce distractions from your work being done. A study was performed on students at the University of Arizona and the University of Washington. These people were placed through eight weeks of mindfulness meditation. During this time, the students had to perform a stressful test demonstrating multitasking before and after the training.

It was shown that those who practiced meditation were able to increase their memory and lower their stress while multitasking.

While mental improvements are fantastic benefits of meditation, physical benefits can help motivate individuals to begin meditation as well. Unfortunately, the standard of health is to turn to medication. If you are an individual who hates popping pills for every issue you have; meditation may be just what you need to help improve your health.

Reduce Risk of Stroke and Heart Disease

It has been found that heart disease is one of the top killers in the world compared to other illnesses. Through meditation, it's possible you could lower your risk of both heart disease and stroke. There was a study done in 2012 for a group of two hundred high-risk people. These individuals were asked to take a class on health, exercise, or take a class on meditation. Over the next five years, it was found that the individuals who chose meditation were able to reduce their risk of death, stroke, and heart attacks by almost half!

Reduce High Blood Pressure

In a clinical study based around meditation, it was also found that certain Zen meditations such as Zazen, has the ability to lower both stress and high blood pressures. It's believed that relaxation response techniques could lower blood pressure levels after three short months of practicing. Through meditation, individuals had less need for medication for their blood pressure! This could potentially be due to the fact that when we relax, it helps open your blood vessels through the formation of nitric oxide.

Live a Longer Life

When you get rid of stress in your life, you may be amazed at how much more energetic and healthier you feel. While the research hasn't been drawn to a conclusion yet, there are some studies that suggest meditation could have an effect on the telomere length in our cells. Telomeres are in charge of how our cells age. When there is less cognitive stress, it helps maintain telomere and other hormonal factors.

There are some people who are looking for a little bit more peace in your life. In the world we live in today, times can be very trying. There are constant deadlines, bills to pay, people to deal with; but now is the time to look at stressors in your life under a different life. Through meditation, you can become a more caring and empathetic individual to create a more peaceful life for yourself.

Improve Positive Relationships and Empathy

When we undergo stressful situations with obnoxious people, it can be very trying to remain empathetic. There is a Buddhist tradition of practicing loving-kindness meditation that may be able to help foster a sense of care toward all living things. Through meditation, you'll be able to boost the way you read facial expressions and gain the ability to empathize with others. When you have a loving attitude toward yourself and others, this helps develop a positive relationship with them and a sense of self-acceptance.

Decrease Feelings of Loneliness

There are many people who are not okay with being alone. Often times, we try to fill our time with activities so that we are never alone with ourselves. The truth is, it can be healthy to spend some time with yourself so that you can self-reflect on your life choices. In a study published in Brain, Behavior, and Immunity, it was proven that after thirty minutes of meditation per day, it was able to reduce individuals' sense of loneliness while reducing the risks of premature death, depression, and perhaps even Alzheimer's.

Along with feeling less lonely, meditation also opens up new doors to feeling a positive connection to yourself. When you love yourself, and you are happy with your own company, you may spend a lot less time on negative thoughts and feelings of self-doubt; both of which can lead to self-caused stress.

Chapter 19 Types of Guided Meditation

Our will power is continuously put through its paces, making it harder to control ourselves in an increasingly chaotic world. Luckily, we are not born with fixed willpower; like anything else, willpower can be cultivated and increased. After all, studies have shown that willpower breeds success. Training the brain with meditation helps fortify your strength (self-control) in dealing with the physical circumstances.

When you practice meditation once a day, every day makes it easier to control your focus, energy, and tenacity when trying new things that require dedication and effort. Guided meditations are designed to help boost our willpower to reduce the negativity in our lives, like stress and bad habits, and focus on love, positive energy, and behaviors. Meditation not only increases willpower, but it also reduces stress and increases our ability to learn.

Concentration Meditation

This practice takes about 15 minutes, and it focuses on concentrating your mind on one thing. On different days, the focus of your mind will be different. You can choose to do the exercise in five, ten, or fifteen minutes.

Sit still with your eyes closed for the proposed length of time and resist the urge to indulge your impulses. When you think you are still is when your body itches- try not to scratch. Do not move, allow the noise and the world around you to continue their flow but do not engage. When time lapses, finish the meditation and acknowledge the stillness you managed to achieve. With time, your mind will learn to remain still and focus on one thing at a time.

Breathing Meditation

This exercise focuses on the feeling of breathing. Close your eyes and inhale. Note "inhale" in your mind, and "exhale" when you breathe out. When your mind wanders off, allow it to label all the other sensations of the body, such as "back itchy," or "sound of dogs barking," etc. You can also ask yourself how it feels to breathe. Is your body relaxing? Can you feel the tension leaving your body? Then pull your mind back to breathing. Allow this rhythmic movement of the mind and thoughts from the breathing pattern, to the sensations.

Breathing meditation will help you become more aware of your environment and assist with impulse control in response to your surroundings. It also activates the brain's prefrontal cortex, quieting the stress and cravings.

Desensitization Using Meditation

This practice is used to control fear, anxiety, stress, anger, and other forms of psychological trauma. It is useful as a healing/ coping tool. This meditation exercise begins with relaxing your body, use relaxation meditation techniques to bring your body and mind to calm. Then, invite your mind into an environment that causes anxiety for you. The situation may cause you anger, distress, uneasy, etc. If the emotions become overwhelming, and it starts to feel less like meditation and more of trauma, return your mind to the feeling of relaxation.

This technique does not always work, especially for fragile people. If you are beginning to heal, it is best to start with other forms of meditation before you try out this practice. However, the exercise helps you handle stressful situations better with what is called "graduated exposure."

Compassion Meditation

Self-compassion is of tremendous importance when making a difficult life change in your life, such as healing from trauma. Self-love will help you overcome challenges that may seem impossible. It involves the repetition of specific phrases that shift the attention from judgment, dislike, and ridicule, to caring, love, and understanding.

In this meditation practice, the instructor will ask you to come up with thoughts and memories when you felt love for yourself, care, happiness, and contentment. You will also be asked to imagine sending thoughts of love, peace, and affection to the people dearest to you. Assume that with every breath you inhale love from them, and exhale love and affection back to them.

Yoga Nidra

This practice takes approximately 30-minutes. It promotes body relaxation while maintaining alertness of the mind. Yoga Nidra is also referred to as dynamic sleep, where the balance between wakefulness and sleep is nurtured.

This form of guided meditation will take you through the active thinking stage, then the relaxing, thoughtless, second stage, the instructor takes you deeper into a third, slowed state of thought. In this state, thinking has been considerably slowed, and it is possible to learn copious amounts of information at this stage (super-learning). Finally, the body and mind enter the last phase, known as the delta stage, where restorative functions happen. Your organs regenerate and heal, and the body releases all the pent-up stress. Do not try to skip the steps as every phase has its purpose, and the therapeutic process will not be reached if parts of the exercise are omitted.

You can practice these techniques one at a time, and do not feel pressured to master them all. If one does not work for you, it is okay, move on to the other. Meditation is not a quick-fix solution; therefore, dedicated practice is necessary for the desired outcome.

The next time you feel downcast or undisciplined, retreat to your meditation and remember that willpower is a muscle, and you have it within yourself. Resisting the power of your thoughts is difficult, but once mastered, you can as quickly learn to overcome other habits and temptations. The more control you gain over your internal turmoil, the better placed you will be to deal with your immediate surroundings. Constant practice will yield gradual improvement as meditation is the most straightforward and effective way to improve willpower.

Chapter 20 What is Meditation?

Meditation is a skill that is acquired through dedicated training of the mind and practice. Meditation is compared to fitness and exercise in relation to body training and overall fitness. The training is inclusive of claims to train the attention or to achieve a calmness or a compassionate mood. The dictionary defines meditation as the deep thinking of something or focusing one's mind for some time on one specific thing without losing focus. Meditation is also defined as the artistic nature of giving attention to one thing, or the engaging in mental exercise to reach a heightened level of spiritual awareness and understanding.

According to psychology, meditation is highly characteristic of its role in attention with an attempt of getting beyond the reflective discursive thinking beyond the logic mind achieving a deeper, more devout and more relaxed state. Another psychologist sees meditation as having a set of self-regulation practices which help to focus on the training attention and awareness to have the mental process under greater voluntary control. It brings forth general mental well-being like calmness, clarity, and concentration. On the other hand, meditation is also viewed as a practice that self regulates the body and mind, hence affecting mental events. Other psychologists define meditation as a stylized mental technique that is practiced in repetition with the main aim of attaining a subjective experience which in mind describing it will be having a very restful, silent, blissful and highly heightened alertness state of mind.

Meditation is, hence, believed to be the acquisition of peace and quietness against everyday stressing life and the opening of doors to the deepest and divine parts of our lives. Meditation helps to train in awareness, thus getting a healthy sense of perspective by learning how to observe your thoughts and feelings without being judgmental on them but instead with time, get to understand them.

Having mentioned that meditation is a skill that means meditation has to be learned, it is reasonable to look at meditation like muscle exercise, which one has not done before. Therefore, for the muscle exercise to work and be comfortable with the body system, one will need to do a lot of practice. To get to a level of comfort, understanding, and doing the right thing, one must have a teacher or a trainer who will guide and help one to do the exercise in knowledge. The ability to learn from a knowledgeable person is key in getting it right, and within a specific time as concerns. There are several people who over the years have learned the art and the skill of meditation and are willing to pass the knowledge to those people who are interested. As such, it is necessary to take advantage of such people and learn more about meditation.

Meditation is a practice that is not always as easy as it may seem. Those who have done it for long will say how when meditating there are times when they will lose focus, and the mind will wander, and consequently cause them to forget to follow the breath.

They say the way the mind loses focus and begins to wander is just part of the memorable experience they are creating. The important part of meditation is consistency and willingness. Meditation, in other words, is termed as one of those things where the journey is what is more important than the destination. Meditation puts more value on the journey, the practice, the commitment, and the dedication employed to achieve a peaceful state of mind.

During meditation, it might take time before your mind gets comfortable to the whole exercise. Chances that setbacks will be present are very high, but the good news is that those setbacks are part of the meditation process. It needs a lot of practice, and just by the fact that you are creating time for the training and learning, is very important in the journey of meditation. One primary invariant ingredient in meditation is the crucial need of the meditator to try and sustain their attention, be it through the concentration or the mindfulness of the whole process. With the retention of concentration achieving the skillful nature, o meditation can be attained.

More often than not, we are controlled and dominated by our thoughts or feelings. Under normal circumstances, we tend to believe we are precisely what those thoughts and feelings say we are. For example, when we have ideas that this is a sad situation, we somehow reflect the sadness on our faces and in the long run we feel anxious and stressed. The same applies to the feeling of joy and happiness. We focus on something as being good then the feeling of satisfaction is reflected on our faces as laughter or a smile. Meditation picks us up by letting us be, giving us a positive experience without any interference of our state of being. Meditation is then concluded to be the natural state of nature, and that is why more than often it is thought that we can read an individual's thoughts by looking at their faces which is a clear reflection of what is their minds or what they are experiencing at that exact moment.

Meditation is made up of different techniques which we shall expand on each later in the teachings. The meditative methods, techniques, or devices are then the means through which we create an intimate personal ambiance which is the facilitation force that disconnects the body and the mind and allows one to be. Of great importance is to set aside time from practicing the meditation techniques and find which method would work well in an everyday life practice context without affecting your work schedule, leisure and your interaction with people at different levels.

Chapter 21 How Does Meditation Work?

To a bystander, a person in the meditative state may look like an idle person sitting in a cross-legged posture with eyes closed. There is no complexity. One doesn't even need to be in this position to meditate. You can meditate while sitting on a chair, while walking or even while lying on the ground.

The body may look inactive while in the meditative state, but the mind is very active. You can unfold some of the most complex mysteries of mind in the meditative state.

On the physical level, meditation strongly influences the activity of the brain. It helps in clearing the mind and also brings objective focus.

Every important thought that comes to your brain leads to a certain type of chemical reaction. The positive thoughts have a calming effect. Happy thoughts lead to the secretion of chemicals that suppress anger and anxiety. When you have a lot of negative, stressful, and fearful thoughts, the production of stress hormones increases in your body. This will not only cause emotional trouble but will also weaken your immune system.

A person trying to lose weight will find it really difficult to burn fat while in a stressful emotional state. The reason being the increased production of the stress hormone. This hormone keeps the body in a constant fat storage mode.

Meditation is a wonderful way to relax your mind as well as the nervous system. It increases activity in the specific regions in the brain associated with decreasing anxiety and depression. Your body also develops a better tolerance for pain. Memory, self-awareness, and the ability of goal setting also improves with the help of meditation.

Our brain in its active state produces beta waves that are fast and choppy. The thoughts in this state can be jumbled up. There are too many thoughts at the same time with very little control over them. However, while in the meditative state, the brain starts producing slow alpha waves. These waves cause relaxation. The stress level starts to go down. The rambling of thought also goes down. You will start feeling greater control over your mind in this state. These waves are associated with feelings of love, positivity, and happiness. The level of alpha waves keeps increasing as one starts to practice meditation for longer.

Meditation can bring physical change in the shape and size of your brain. Studies conducted on long-time practitioners have demonstrated that meditation leads to an increase in the gray matter in certain areas of the brain.

Two important areas are:

Insular Cortex: This area is associated with an awareness of breathing and heartbeat. The longer you meditate the better will be your breathing and heart. This would mean that your body would be in a better position to carry oxygen and carbon dioxide. You would have better immunity against diseases.

Premotor Cortex: This area regulates attention, emotions, and thoughts. Your learning power and memory would also improve if the gray matter in this area gets denser. You would have better control over your emotions and thoughts.

The Amygdala in your brain deals with stress, fear, and anxiety. Studies have clearly demonstrated that meditation can help in decreasing the gray matter in this area. It can greatly help in reducing stress, fear, high blood pressure, and immunity-related disorders.

With practice, your brain can also start producing gamma waves. These waves can help in bringing deep concentration and an unwavering focus.

Apart from the physiological stuff, meditation also helps you in developing better ability to deal with your thoughts and emotions.

Our mind remains mostly confused between wants and needs. The problems begin when it starts treating both interchangeably. Our expectations from people, jobs, relationships, personal wealth, and other such things are always high and when they aren't met, we start having negative thoughts.

Meditation helps you in viewing your thoughts objectively. You will be able to understand the true value of things and also judge the futility of wants. This can make life much simpler. Most of the things that deem essential are not even required in life, but we waste our lives pursuing them. We simply follow them endlessly because we see others around us doing the same. We acquire the herd mentality and get involved in the mind-numbing rat race. Meditation helps you in objectively analyzing our thoughts, needs, and wants to choose the best course of action.

You'd find yourself much more calm, relaxed, and peaceful after meditation sessions. Decision making would become easier and your mind wouldn't be constantly battling decision fatigue. Your perspective about things would improve along with your ability to look at things objectively.

Chapter 22 Why Practice Meditation?

1. It Turns You into A Better Decision-maker

One of the main problems of making a habit out of DMN is that you think that you only have limited choices to make decisions. Rather than considering if something can be good (or bad), you just act on whatever things might come by default. The more you subject yourself to this habit of yours, the more ingrained in your mind it becomes, until such time comes when you do it without even thinking about your best interests.

2. It Provides You with A Place Where You Can Be Free from Conditioning

How many times have you watched the evening news and there always seem to be at least one news item that grinds your gears? It is quite unfortunate that most people go through life reactively. Mindfulness provides you with awareness and a space in your head that allows you to choose how to respond, rather than having a knee-jerk reaction to things. You get a chance to choose your reaction rather than letting your mind default to the kinds of reactions that society has ingrained into you.

3. It Allows You to Increase Your Emotional Intelligence

Medical studies have shown that people who practice mindfulness have better control over their emotions compared to other people. In fact, the US Military conducted their own research on mindfulness and how it could help sufferers of PTSD. Their research yielded that mindfulness can actually help minimize stress, and even ease the effects of chronic stress.

Mindfulness training not only makes you more mature emotionally, you also gain more empathy, compassion, and you also become more altruistic. After even just eight weeks, you will feel more empathy with others, and you are also more able to take compassionate action.

4. It Helps Your Body Thrive

Mindfulness can also increase the amount of physical activity that your body can endure. Most people distract themselves from their workouts, but it is actually better when you practice mindfulness while you are working out. For instance, if you are in a hurry to finish your weight training workout, you will only focus on doing the requisite number of repetitions, and not pay attention to your form. And when you are not careful about your lifting form, you are more prone to getting seriously injured. With mindfulness, not only are you careful about your weightlifting form, you will also feel more accomplished with every set that you complete.

5. It Helps You Become More Creative

Creativity arises from the DMN. In these periods of unfocused rest, you have the chance to have a different perspective, you can make new associations between ideas and strike upon them. For instance, if you are a sculptor, you do not immediately know what to carve out of a huge chunk of stone. You need to sit in front of that huge slab of stone and visualize what you can make out of it. The only way to see the final sculpture clearly is to eliminate all distractions around you.

With mindfulness, you can say goodbye to all of your distractions, and say hello to an almost infinite source of inspiration.

6. It Helps Strengthen Existing Neural Connections and Build New Ones

Mindfulness can actually reshape the human brain, it meant in terms of creating new neural connections. Practicing mindfulness as often as you can cause your brain to build new neural pathways, and ultimately new neural networks, thus making it function more efficiently. This helps your brain by improving concentration and awareness.

7. What Do You Need to Do to be More Mindful?

Practice mindfulness ad nauseam. There is no shortcut or magic pill that will help you become instantly more mindful. Instant results are not promised, although you will receive tips that will make the process much easier, but it will still take you some time before you can become fully mindful. Being mindful means that you are training your mind to be aware of what it is thinking, rather than becoming what it is actually thinking.

This is where meditation can help you. There are many ways to meditate, the traditional method of sitting in a quiet place and observing your thoughts without being judgmental is the easiest way and is also the best place to start for beginners. It might sound simple, but the problem is that most people are not living in the present, they are constantly worrying about things that are yet to happen or happened already. Your thoughts are constantly running around uncontrolled in your brain. With mindfulness, you can put a bit of space around your thoughts so you can easily let go of comparisons, judgments, and control of them.

Chapter 23 Best Meditation Techniques

Meditation in itself is a simple and great way to bring better clarity in mind and attain greater peace. All meditation techniques take you towards these goals. Various meditation techniques followed these days have been designed to achieve this objective. The only difference is in the way they help you in doing them.

It would be unfair to say that one technique is better than the other as the objective of all the techniques is the same. They all have the potential to deliver the results. You must choose a technique that suits you the most. The technique in which you are most comfortable would be the best. One that works for others might not work for you. Therefore, it is important that you choose a technique in which you are most comfortable and find your rhythm.

Some of the most popular meditation techniques are:

Breathing and Relaxation Meditation

This is the easiest form of meditation best for beginners. In this meditation, you will have to focus on your breathing and that would help you in relaxing the body. This meditation helps greatly in releasing tension from various parts of the body and also helps in relieving stress and anxiety. You can do it at your home without any guide or supervision. This meditation can also be done whenever you are feeling anxious, stressed, or angry.

1. Mindfulness

It is one of the most popular forms of meditation being practiced in the west these days. It doesn't bound you with particular settings or restrictions of time and place. You can do it anywhere anytime. The most important aspect of this meditation is to be mindful of all the thoughts entering your mind. You don't need to restrain your thoughts or train your mind to think in a particular way. You simply need to observe the kind of thoughts you are having. This meditation helps you in thinking objectively. You also get a chance to look at your thoughts in a non-judgmental way and understand their root cause. It is one of the best ways to suppress anger and stress.

2. Loving-Kindness Meditation

It is a form of Buddhist meditation and is also known as Metta meditation. It is a wonderful meditation for people who always feel agitated and have sudden anger outbursts. If negative thoughts and depression and making your life difficult then this meditation can help you a lot. In this meditation, you direct love, kindness, and gratitude toward yourself and the people around you. This meditation helps you in addressing your anger and you develop the ability to manage your sudden anger outbursts more effectively.

3. Body Scan Meditation

This is a great way to meditate if you want to relax your body completely. It gives you a chance to feel each and every part of your body and observe the sensations closely. It will relax you completely and instill a feeling of wellness. You can do this meditation in standing, sitting, or lying positions. It is easy to do and can be followed for around half hours daily for best results.

4. Mantra Meditation

It is a great way to shun all thoughts and focus your mind on a particular sound. Mantra meditation is a very popular practice and is very effective in bringing calmness. You will be able to shun thoughts and focus your mind on one sound, place, or object. Every mantra has unique vibrations that focus your mind on one thing. This meditation is very effective if you want to meditate for longer periods and maintaining an unwavering focus is very easy through mantra meditation.

5.   Chakra Meditation

This meditation practice originated in India. It works on the principle that our body is divided into various energy circles with each circle having its unique role. Indian mythology says that when these energy chakras are out of sync, there are physical as well as mental problems. Through this meditation, all these energy chakras are activated, and a balance is sought. Every chakra has its own color and can be activated through specific sound vibrations. You can follow guided meditations for chakra awakening for faster results.

6.   Third Eye Meditation

The third eye is the sixth chakra in our body also known as 'Ajna' chakra. This chakra dominates our intellect and also controls our sixth sense as well as our psychic abilities. Third Eye meditation helps in awakening this chakra and honing the psychic abilities. If getting greater spiritual consciousness is your goal, then also this is a great form of meditation for you.

7.   Gazing Meditation

This meditation is used for bringing greater focus on things. This is an externally focused meditation and requires you to focus on physical objects like a candle, painting, dots, and other such things. You will have to gaze at the objects and hold their mental images in your eyes. This practice can help in relaxing the mind completely. The mind gets absorbed in the process to such an extent that all other thoughts causing agitation or anger pass away. You can do this meditation anytime.

8. Zazen or Zen

It is a Buddhist meditation practice. It helps in relaxing your body, mind, and soul. It isn't a religious practice but a spiritual one. You can follow it irrespective of your religion. It is done while sitting in a cross-legged posture with the eyes closed.

The first part of this meditation is to sit straight in a fixed position. You keep your body straight yet relaxed. This helps in taking away all the stress.

The second part of the meditation is controlled breathing. You will have to keep your breathing focused. This relaxes your mind completely. It drives away all the racing thoughts.

The third part is to bring your thoughts in line with your body. As you meditate, you start getting better control over your thoughts and emotions.

9. Guided Meditation

Guided meditations are the best if you want to meditate regularly but don't have the time to go to a guru or a teacher. With the help of the instructions and imagery given through guided meditation, you will be able to meditate in a much better way. It is a very easy and convenient way to meditate in the comfort of your home or office. You can use guided meditation for all types of meditations mentioned above.

Chapter 24 Guided Mindful Meditation for Anxiety

Reducing Anxiety Around Wins and Regrets

Time: 5 to 15 minutes

In this exercise, you'll focus specifically on what we call wins and regrets. We all have things that we are working on, positive habits we want to strengthen and negative ones we wish to eliminate. Our awareness of, efforts towards, and results with these things can all be anxiety-provoking, especially if we are not succeeding. This exercise is designed to assist you in this area and reduce your anxiety.

Steps

1. Find a comfortable place where you won't be disturbed but won't fall asleep. Sit comfortably but remain alert. Focus on your breathing, becoming mindful and letting your mind settle. Remain in that state for a minute or two.

2. Think about the goals you have set for yourself, and those you are working on; both things that you want to achieve, as well as things to eliminate. Take 1 to 2 minutes to do this.

3. Now, review your day with these two areas in mind, noting where you won and where you have regrets.

4. Think about the successes, while remaining mindful and relaxed, and let yourself enjoy the positive, good feelings that go with that. Enjoy that for 1 to 2 minutes.

5. Next, recall the regrets that came out of the day, and notice what those feel like. See if you can inquire into what happened, and where things went wrong or fell short. Notice how you think about it, breathing into and through the unpleasant emotions or sensations. Note if any amends or reparations might be in order, or if you need to alter your strategy and be more mindful around certain things. Do mindfulness meditation on all of this for 2 to 3 minutes.

6. Remember that tomorrow is another day, and you will have a chance to improve. Try and let all anxiety and stress go.

7. Sit for a few minutes, in regular mindfulness meditation, letting go of all those things that you were working on. Return to your breath, just focusing on the respiration, and allow yourself to calm and settle as you wind down for the evening.

Reduce Negative Thinking to Reduce Anxiety

Time: 10 to 15 minutes

The way we think, positively or negatively, has a massive impact on our emotions, and by changing our negative thinking, we can allay our anxieties.

We are mentally talking to ourselves, whether we are conscious of it or not, almost all of the time. Unfortunately, we are often saying some very negative and scary things, with the result being an enormous amount of anxiety. It's time to change that.

Steps

1. Find a quiet, comfortable place to sit, with back straight and relaxed. Find your breath at the nostrils and follow it for a couple of minutes as you settle.

2. Think of something that causes you a lot of anxiety. Go over the story around this thing, and as you do, begin to notice the thoughts that go along with it.

3. Pay particular attention to the negative thoughts, and how you feel when you have these thoughts. Take several minutes to do this.

4. Choose one or two of the main negative thoughts and examine them. Look and see if these cynical, anxiety-provoking thoughts are really accurate and supported by data. Do this for 1 to 2 minutes.

5. Notice what you found; most of our negative and anxiety-provoking thoughts have no immediate basis in reality. There is no one holding a gun to your head or about to run you over, and you are not dying this very moment. This is an important discovery to make. Take 1 to 2 minutes to examine this.

6. Feel the feelings that are behind all of these serious, scary thoughts. There are things that we are afraid of and that we have not dealt with emotionally. Now is the time to do that. Take 3 to 5 minutes and breathe into the fear that is behind the scary thoughts. Feel a bit of the emotion, find the physical sensation that goes with it, and direct the breath into and through it.

7. Some underlying fears should begin to subside, though grave underlying concerns may need to be worked with in this way many times.

8. After some of the underlying fear has been lessened, go back, review the negative thoughts, and change them to something that is at least neutral, if not positive. Take a couple minutes to do this.

9. 9Return to the simple mindfulness meditation for at least a couple of minutes while you settle, make a few notes, and return to your day.

10. 10You can benefit from doing this exercise more than once for recurring issues or whenever negative self-talk arises. Do this as often as you need or like.

Plan Ahead to Reduce Anxiety

Time: 5 to 20 minutes

If you think about it, you may realize that a lot of your anxiety is tied up in thoughts about the future; things you dread either happening or not happening, and it may also be related to painful events from the past. Since so much worry is directed at the future and negative things happening, one beneficial way to deal with anxiety is to plan for the future you want. You can do this meditation as a future planning exercise or when you're having anxious thoughts.

Steps

1. Find a comfortable place where you won't be disturbed, settle in, and begin to follow your breath. Bring something to write with.

2. Think about and review the sorts of fears and worries that you have about your future. Notice if it's about your health, wealth, relationships, work, or something else.

3. Try to identify the main one or two things causing you the most worry about your future.

4. Notice the main worry thoughts and feel the fear regarding what you dread for the future. Allow yourself to breathe into and through the fearful emotion and any related sensations. Stay with this for a while and see if it begins to relax and shift.

5. From this more settled and clearer place, think about how you would like your future to be. Think about what things you want to have happen instead of what you fear.

6. Lay out a plan as to how you can create the outcome that you want, instead of reacting to and avoiding the result that you fear. Later you may want to write this down.

7. What is an action step you can take right now towards realizing the future that you want? Visualize taking that step.

8. Recognize that you are either actively envisioning and creating the future that you want or fearing and worrying about that which you don't want. The choice is yours.

9. Sit for a moment, return to the easy breath, settle, come out of the meditation, and return to your daily life.

10. Build these review and action steps into your daily life, at least for a while.

Chapter 25 Guided Meditation for Sleep

Mindful Bedtime Meditation

Time: 5 minutes

Anxious people often have difficulty going to bed early. This difficulty can be due to the internal energy buzz, or a worrying mind that is turning and spinning, but regardless, they have considerable difficulty choosing a reasonable bedtime and adhering to it. Going to bed earlier and getting more and better sleep can significantly reduce anxiety, as well as improve overall health, focus, and our ability to follow through and be productive.

Steps

1. Find a comfortable place to relax and settle, while you lightly enter into mindfulness meditation.

2. Think about what the ideal bedtime for you might be, taking into consideration your age, health, nutrition, workload, and any other relevant factors. The first time you do this, you may need to be more formal and extensive as you figure this out. Be sure to include such things as what the ideal time for you is to wake and get up the next day, especially considering your schedule.

Take 1 to 3 minutes to do this. In the future, you can likely do this in 30 seconds to 1 minute.

3. Now, think about what usually gets in the way of your adhering to this bedtime—maybe such things as binge-watching a series on Netflix, getting involved in activities on the Internet, exercising too late, eating too late and feeling uncomfortable, or a myriad of other things. Think about what your usual nemesis is. Take 2 to 3 minutes to do this. In the future, it may require less than 1 minute.

4. Return to the mindfulness meditation, watching and following the breath, as you note any significant reactions to what you found. Think about actually planning to go to bed on time and sticking to it. Imagine and feel that for a minute or two.

5. Plan out the rest of your evening to follow the script that you laid out, and take 1 to 2 minutes to do that, as you continue with your mindfulness meditation, then finish your evening.

6. Hopefully, you will follow the script, and get yourself to bed earlier, reducing your stress and increasing your ease and focus.

7. If something else happens, make a note of it and factor it into the next time that you do this exercise. You may want to keep records of this, such as writing sleep times in your calendar or using an app to keep track.

Chill Out: A Sleepy Meditation

Time: 5 to 20 minutes

This is one of my favorite meditations for late evening or if I need a short nap during the day.

In our usual meditation, we sit reasonably upright, eyes often open, and focus on remaining quite alert. This meditation exercise is best done in or near bed, often slouching, and with eyes usually closed. You want to calm down and settle your mind, avoid revving back up, and encourage yourself to move into sleep. If it's during the day, you could choose a comfortable chair, slump down in it, and let your eyes close.

Steps

1. Find a quiet and comfortable place where you can really relax and let go. Make sure you have no place to be for at least 20 to 30 minutes. If it is daytime, you may want to set an alarm.

2. Sit very comfortably, likely slouched, and let your eyes close. Focus on your breath and let yourself really settle and relax. Take 2 to 5 minutes to do this.

3. Don't try to keep your eyes open, and don't try to sit up straight. Get as comfortable as you can and let yourself relax and let go as much as you can.

4. If thoughts or other things try to arise, just barely notice them and let them go, and keep returning to moving towards dozing and/or sleeping. Take as long as you need.

5. At some point, you will likely begin to doze off. This is a good thing and should not be avoided or resisted. Just keep letting yourself go, taking as long as you need.

6. If it's daytime, when you awaken or your alarm goes off, take a moment to slowly rouse yourself, breathe mindfully for about a minute, and then return to your day.

7. If it's nighttime, you can adjust your pillow and slide down into your comfortable bed, letting yourself continue off to sleep.

Insomnia: Tips and a Restful Meditation

Time: 10 minutes to an hour or more

Insomnia is a condition that most people experience at some time in their life. Occasional difficulty going to sleep, such as before a big event or medical procedure, is not uncommon and not much cause for concern. It's the regular, ongoing difficulty falling asleep that is problematic and concerning. It can result in depression or anxiety, weight gain, cognitive clouding, immune system suppression, and decreased motivation. Some people have insomnia related to sleep apnea, a condition that can have serious medical implications. Check with your doctor to rule out any medical basis for your insomnia.

I strongly suggest avoiding caffeine or other stimulants, especially after 2 p.m., as this can affect your ability to sleep later.

A regular bedtime that's not too late is best. Also recommended are measures like slowing down in the evening, avoiding stimulation, putting away the electronics, not exercising vigorously or overeating in the evening, and keeping the room dark and not too warm. Failing to follow these measures can lead to a heightened arousal state of the nervous system and make sleep very difficult. If you are prone to insomnia, I suggest doing this meditation before you try to go to sleep.

Steps

1. If you have tried the approaches listed in the introduction and still can't sleep, your insomnia is likely driven by anxiety. You can verify this by noticing the incessant worrying thoughts. Take a minute or two to become aware of this.

2. Lie on your side and get comfortable. I prefer lying on my right side with the left nostril up, as breathing through the left nostril is less stimulating. While lying on your side, do the basic mindfulness meditation, with an even in and out and a slightly longer exhalation. Do this for 5 to 10 minutes.

3. Find what body area stands out the most and imagine directing your respiration into and through it. Continue for as long as you need to and come back into it as needed. Ideally, your mind will slow down, things will shift, and you will ease off to sleep.

4. If you are unable to actually fall asleep, at least you will be getting rest, though not deep sleep. Continue with this as long as you need to.

5. Some sleep specialists recommend getting up to read or watch TV, but something light and not action-packed, instead of lying

in bed and worrying about not being able to sleep. Keep the lights low. Writing your thoughts can also be helpful—whether it's a to-do list or a problem to solve—writing it down can transfer ownership from your head to the paper, clearing your mind. Often you can then go back to bed and sleep.

6. If the insomnia is frequent and severe, I strongly suggest that you consult with your medical doctor.

Get Back to Sleep

Time: 2 to 15 minutes

Waking up in the night is another unpleasant sleep issue. If your waking up is due to needing to use the bathroom, and you quickly fall back asleep, then it's really no problem. It's when you wake up and have a hard time falling back asleep that it's a real issue. Usually, when this happens, we've awakened with a start, and there is a strong emotion, upsetting thoughts, or a combination of the two. This situation is what we will focus on for this meditation.

Steps

1. When you wake up unexpectedly the middle of the night or early morning, turn on your side and begin the basic mindfulness meditation. Focus your attention on the breath and do this for 2 to 3 minutes. This simple approach may result in you going back to sleep.

2. If the wakeful state persists, become aware of the primary emotion and sensation associated with it. Focus your attention on that as you breathe into and through it. You can do this for as long as you need to, though it will often shift within 5 to 10 minutes, and you will ease back into sleep. Repeat this as necessary.

3. If it still persists, add some of the cognitive approach and question whether your fearful thoughts are accurate. Continue directing the breath into and through the experience.

4. If all else fails, you may wish to get up for a while to stretch lightly, walk around a bit, journal, read a book, or even watch something light on TV until you can settle enough to go back to sleep.

Chapter 26 Guided Meditation for Good and Happy Wake Up

Guide Meditation for Super Motivation

At times we need to find the cause of motivation for us to keep doing some things. Take, for instance, an individual who works for long hours. They have to find things that motivate them to get up each morning.

If you are asked what your reason for living is, what would you have to say? What is that one thing that makes you want to try harder without giving up? There is some power that results from motivation. It allows us to want to do better in the activities that we undertake.

It makes us have meaning in what we go. One of the best ways to stay motivated is to have goals that you want to accomplish. In this case, the goal is to lose weight.

As an individual, you have to ensure that you are focused on that goal for it to be effective. If you wish to cut off some extra weight, get something that inspires you. For instance, you can be inspired to weigh a certain amount. In that process, you can be evaluating how much you way daily and how far away you are from getting to your goal.

Hypnosis is a great way to help those in need of weight loss. There are various reasons a person may be overweight. Some may range from behavioral issues or underlying conditions that will require to be addressed to lose weight successfully. In this chapter, we will take you through a guide for a weight loss program through hypnosis as well as how to lose weight through meditation. After losing weight, a person needs to maintain it. We shall further discuss how hypnosis can help one maintain their new weight and avoid becoming overweight again.

A person needs a lot of help and motivation to succeed. With the help of hypnotherapy, one can easily stay the course and watch the pounds melt away. Following the guide above and with a credible hypnotherapist or mastering self-hypnosis will help you in achieving your goals.

For any get-healthy plan to work, it begins with shaping an association with nourishment. When they must be aware of how they eat, why they eat, and the health benefit of what they eat. The motivation behind trance for weight reduction is to empower an individual to be aware of their eating examples and nourishments to have a fruitful adventure in weight reduction.

At times fear motivates us into doing certain things. For instance, you might fear to get obese or acquiring some lifestyle diseases. Such fear ensures that you stay focused on losing weight. You ensure that you strictly follow your diet plan or that you exercise regularly. Instead of fear motivating you negatively, it motivates you in a positive way. Another case example is the fear we have before taking tests or exams.

The fear of potentially failing can make you burn the midnight oil to ensure that you do not fail in the tasks that you have engaged in.

You find yourself trying to do your best in the various tasks that you are undertaking. Eventually, you may pass in your test, with fear as the motivating factor of success. All you need to do is ensure that you convert that energy into something useful and helpful in your life. At times the fear of failure in life makes us work hard towards making a better living. This makes you wake up very early each day, determined to make that day better than the previous day. It ensures that you give your best in life for you to live well.

We, at times, find our motivation from other people. At times you find that you may not be able to inspire yourself enough, but you feel inspired by other people. When you are unable to walk alone, you can always seek help from individuals that are more inspired than you are.

They ensure that you are always working hard towards achieving your goals and that you do not deviate from other things.

This type of motivation is positive and useful in your life. It ensures that you give your best in the activities that you undertake. Walking alone can, at times, be challenging.

Anytime you feel like giving up, and there is no one to remind you why you started the journey in the first place. You are prone to making wrong decisions that you will end up regretting.

One needs to have individuals that encourage them in the journey they take. As you start your weight loss journey through meditation, you can look for an individual with the same goal. You get to keep encouraging each other to accomplish certain things, and it becomes easier to achieve the set goals.

Guide Meditation for Boost Positivity

You need to shed off any unimportant attachment.

Unimportant attachments are things that no longer have any effect on your life.

These are things that will only let you down, thus derailing your life goals of achieving a mind-set full of happiness. Your future success depends heavily on this, and for you to get at that position, you will need to detach yourself from anything that might let you down. You must note that anything might also mean any person.

We have people in our lives that always try very hard to put us down. These types of people are afraid of your success in life.

They will try their best to pull you down, no matter how hard you try to embrace only positivity in your life. It is time to get yourself going and void them like the plague. Remember, you must live and not only live but choose a pleasant experience.

It will only be possible if you manage to refuse anything or anyone that is holding you back. Since I have said this, it is now my wish that you may practice this affirmation and use it as your routine daily. Practice makes perfect, and you will only realize that when you train.

You are enough just as you are. You must release that demonic notion of having comparisons between you and others. For you to stay specific, you must have some success standards. After developing all these, set your own goals and ambitions. Your vision should relate to your mission in life. After all these, you can now judge yourself using the basis of your success.

Those rules and regulations you created in your success standards should enable you to judge yourself accordingly. Just know you are just enough the way you were born. You are a complete soul, and no part of you is lacking. So never try to make a comparison with others.

You should note that affirmation helps in the realization of worthiness. Within a short period, you will be able to control your body image. Also, it will be of a great deal as it helps you in achieving some of the personal goals in life and having a sound body is one of them.

You must be in a position to fulfill your purpose. The world should know your existence, and you must be ready to show your achievement. Showing your accomplished goals will need some positive deeds that lead to a successful life. On most occasions, people who trend are our trendsetters.

They trend because of having done something positive or negative. They are then known all over the world. However, in this motivational affirmation, you need to focus on positive things.

You need to be a trendsetter in showing the whole world what you are capable of offering. If you have been employed somewhere to sweep, you must clean until the country president cuts short his journey to congratulate you. Achieving your best is always one decisive way to be successful and lead a happy life free from stress and distress. Remember, this affirmation reminds you that no one has that power to stop you from doing or rather fulfilling your purpose in life. Sharing this thought every morning when you wake up will eventually get you somewhere. You must now stay focus and have this habit of telling yourself that no one can prevent you from achieving.

You must be results-oriented. In your daily life, you need to stay focus in life. Your primary focus should be on your results. It is through this that you will be able to realize your productivity.

To achieve this, you must be able to create some space for success. Get more success in your life. Avoid any derailing excuses that will only demean your reputation, thus lowering your success rate. Offer yourself these phrases every morning, and you will be in great joy for the rest of the day. You need not hold on excuses for failing to achieve something. Be yourself and have the ability to struggle until you reach that success in life. It is through this that your mind will have settled, giving you peace of mind. Peace of mind will enable you to lead a stress-free experience. It will reflect in your body image.

Be control of your won happiness. Happiness is an aspect of life that will initiate your feelings and moods towards a positive experience.

It is like a gear geared towards your prosperous life. Staying positive here will be of great importance, and for you to realize this, you must take control of your happiness. Responsibility is a virtue and being responsible will make you bold enough to face all kinds of situations. Your joy is your key to success, and no one should tamper with it. Make happiness your priority and be responsible for it.

You must let no one make you angry. Angriness will only induce you with emotional feelings that will eventually affect your life more so your body image. Having seen this, you must now be in an excellent position to embrace this affirmation. Take it as an opener to your morning and employ it entirely in your life.

To achieve much in this process of weight loss, you need to embark on areas that give you a clear view of affirmations. Remember, affirmations are just phrases that are highly powerful and lead to positivity in life. By applying these affirmations, be sure that you will be able to stay focus, positive, and relaxed. There are several affirmations that you need to choose from. Try picking the ones you can manage and start your daily routine of making them permanent. Your weight will reduce tremendously.

We also aims at making you stay positive about yourself. That's, it indulges you in the world of motivation. Motivational affirmations, therefore, help you in achieving this ultimate goal, thus resulting in a more positive life with lots of happiness and relaxation. Stay tuned once more to these phrases, especially the way they been explained in this chapter. I hope you do prefer a perfect body image full of pleasure and positivity. Imagine a life full of happiness just because you have followed and fully implemented the principles in this book.

Chapter 27 Spiritual Sound for Meditation

This meditation is one of my favorites and I find that a lot of people feel in tuned with it. During this practice, we are going to imagine to be a rock-solid mountain, surrounded by nature and habited by animals, plants and trees.

Once the image is well painted inside our mind, we will add the element of time, allowing it to pass in a constant and smooth way. We are going to feel the different seasons, starting from the Summer, and we are going to experience different emotions. What it is important to notice is how the mountain remains still and solid, even during the most difficult times, offering a safe place for animals and plants.

By becoming self-aware of our mountain-ness, we can face daily difficulties with new energy and a rejuvenated spirit. Doing this practice once a week for a month is ideal to see the most benefits. Also, as you will see it is a pretty interesting and fun experience!

Let's get started!

Find a comfortable, relaxed and balanced position. Give yourself permission to be completely present for yourself, and let your body and mind calm down until they become soft and relaxed.

Breathe in, feel relaxed...

breathe out, feel calm...

Breathe in, feel relaxed...

breathe out, feel calm...

Breathe in, feel relaxed...

breathe out, feel calm...

Breathe in, feel relaxed...

breathe out, feel calm...

Allow the mind to distance itself from all thoughts and orientate awareness on your breath. Breathe naturally and do not force a specific rhythm. Let your breath come and go.

Carefully, now, drive your attention from the breath to the space in which you are.

Feel the energy and atmosphere of this space as it permeates all of your being. Notice the noises in the background. Maybe there is a clock ticking, maybe there are cars passing just outside your windows. Whatever you feel it is fine, let your attention rest on the external.

Breathe in, feel relaxed...

breathe out, feel calm...

Breathe in, feel relaxed...

breathe out, feel calm...

Breathe in, feel relaxed...

breathe out, feel calm...

Breathe in, feel relaxed...

breathe out, feel calm...

Now bring the attention back to the breath. Take your time and you will naturally reach a place of warmth and ease.

There is nothing to do here, nothing to think or to worry about. Just rest your attention on the breath, following each inhalation and exhalation with curiosity, falling into the rhythm of your very own body.

If you want, you can place your hands on your belly. This will help you enter in connection with the natural movement of the air entering through your nose and exciting trough the mouth.

Breathe in, feel relaxed...

breathe out, feel calm...

Breathe in, feel relaxed...

breathe out, feel calm...

Breathe in, feel relaxed...

breathe out, feel calm...

Breathe in, feel relaxed...

breathe out, feel calm...

Breathe in, feel relaxed...

breathe out, feel calm...

Breathe in, feel relaxed...

breathe out, feel calm...

Breathe in, feel relaxed...

breathe out, feel calm...

Breathe in, feel relaxed...

breathe out, feel calm...

I will give you a few more minutes to get into this zone, as we will than begin the actual practice.

Breathe in, feel relaxed...

breathe out, feel calm...

Breathe in, feel relaxed...

breathe out, feel calm...

Breathe in, feel relaxed...

breathe out, feel calm...

Breathe in, feel relaxed...

breathe out, feel calm...

Breathe in, feel relaxed...

breathe out, feel calm...

Breathe in, feel relaxed...

breathe out, feel calm...

Breathe in, feel relaxed...

breathe out, feel calm...

Breathe in, feel relaxed...

breathe out, feel calm...

Breathe in, feel relaxed...

breathe out, feel calm...

Breathe in, feel relaxed...

breathe out, feel calm...

Breathe in, feel relaxed...

breathe out, feel calm...

Breathe in, feel relaxed...

breathe out, feel calm...

Breathe in, feel relaxed...

breathe out, feel calm...

Breathe in, feel relaxed...

breathe out, feel calm...

Breathe in, feel relaxed...

breathe out, feel calm...

Breathe in, feel relaxed...

breathe out, feel calm...

Now start imagining a mountain, a big and rock-solid mountain. If you have a favorite one, you can picture it as well. Maybe it is a place where you go on a regular basis or maybe it is a mountain you have only see on video. Just take a few minutes to paint it as clearly as you can in your mind. Try to grasp every detail, from the height to the temperature. The more you can add, the greater the benefits.

Breathe in, feel relaxed...

breathe out, feel calm...

Breathe in, feel relaxed...

breathe out, feel calm...

Breathe in, feel relaxed...

breathe out, feel calm...

Breathe in, feel relaxed...

breathe out, feel calm...

Breathe in, feel relaxed...

breathe out, feel calm...

Breathe in, feel relaxed...

breathe out, feel calm...

Breathe in, feel relaxed...

breathe out, feel calm...

Breathe in, feel relaxed...

breathe out, feel calm...

Once you have the image in your mind, we can get started. It is Summer and all the animals are coming towards you, finding peace under the shadow you provide them. Tourists and hikers take pictures of you and their kids run up and down your trails. Trees and flowers are nourished by your soil and paint you in a dark green color. Everything is perfect, nice and cozy, and it seems that this beautiful feeling will never end.

Breathe in, feel relaxed...

breathe out, feel calm...

Breathe in, feel relaxed...

breathe out, feel calm...

Breathe in, feel relaxed...

breathe out, feel calm...

Breathe in, feel relaxed...

breathe out, feel calm...

Breathe in, feel relaxed...

breathe out, feel calm...

Breathe in, feel relaxed...

breathe out, feel calm...

Breathe in, feel relaxed...

breathe out, feel calm...

Breathe in, feel relaxed...

breathe out, feel calm...

Breathe in, feel relaxed...

breathe out, feel calm...

Breathe in, feel relaxed...

breathe out, feel calm...

Breathe in, feel relaxed...

breathe out, feel calm...

Breathe in, feel relaxed...

breathe out, feel calm...

Breathe in, feel relaxed...

breathe out, feel calm...

Breathe in, feel relaxed...

breathe out, feel calm...

Breathe in, feel relaxed...

breathe out, feel calm...

Breathe in, feel relaxed...

breathe out, feel calm...

Time goes by very quickly though and sooner than later fewer and fewer people come and take picture of you. The beautiful trees are now losing their leaves and the animals are seeking repair in the valley, leaving you almost alone. The last flowers are perishing, and your soil is not a good source of nourishment anymore. You think that this feeling will never end.

Breathe in, feel relaxed...

breathe out, feel calm...

Breathe in, feel relaxed...

breathe out, feel calm...

Breathe in, feel relaxed...

breathe out, feel calm...

Breathe in, feel relaxed...

breathe out, feel calm...

Breathe in, feel relaxed...

breathe out, feel calm...

Breathe in, feel relaxed...

breathe out, feel calm...

Breathe in, feel relaxed...

breathe out, feel calm...

Breathe in, feel relaxed...

breathe out, feel calm...

Now Winter comes and snow starts coming down, covering all your trails and rocks. There are no flowers popping up and trees are now completely brown. Their leaves are on the ground, covered by snow. The temperature is freezing, and all the animals are now far away, trying to survive this season as best as they can. People stay far away from you, because they are scared of avalanches. They look at you with a deep sense of respect but are not willing to visit you for the time being. You think that this feeling will never end.

Breathe in, feel relaxed...

breathe out, feel calm...

Breathe in, feel relaxed...

breathe out, feel calm...

Breathe in, feel relaxed...

breathe out, feel calm...

Breathe in, feel relaxed...

breathe out, feel calm...

Breathe in, feel relaxed...

breathe out, feel calm...

Breathe in, feel relaxed...

breathe out, feel calm...

Breathe in, feel relaxed...

breathe out, feel calm...

Breathe in, feel relaxed...

breathe out, feel calm...

Slowly things start to change, and you are noticing it with new hope. The snow is melting, the trees becoming green again and beautiful wildflowers are popping up all over you. Soon enough, the first hikers are taking picture of you again and everyone is telling how gorgeous you are. The sun is getting brighter, days are getting longer. Animals are coming back and are dancing for you on your beautiful trails. It is Spring at its finest and you think that this feeling will never end.

Breathe in, feel relaxed...

breathe out, feel calm...

Breathe in, feel relaxed...

breathe out, feel calm...

Breathe in, feel relaxed...

breathe out, feel calm...

Breathe in, feel relaxed...

breathe out, feel calm...

Breathe in, feel relaxed...

breathe out, feel calm...

Breathe in, feel relaxed...

breathe out, feel calm...

Breathe in, feel relaxed...

breathe out, feel calm...

Breathe in, feel relaxed...

breathe out, feel calm...

And in a blink of an eye, everything starts all over again. Summer, Fall, Winter, Spring and then Summer again, in a never-ending cycle. And no matter what happens around you, you are still there, feeling strong and solid as a mountain.

I would like you to bring this feeling with you for the rest of the week, as you are truly capable of amazing things, when you tap into the unlimited source of energy that is your soul.

Breathe in, feel relaxed...

breathe out, feel calm...

Breathe in, feel relaxed...

breathe out, feel calm...

Breathe in, feel relaxed...

breathe out, feel calm...

Breathe in, feel relaxed...

breathe out, feel calm...

Breathe in, feel relaxed...

breathe out, feel calm...

Breathe in, feel relaxed...

breathe out, feel calm...

Breathe in, feel relaxed...

breathe out, feel calm...

Breathe in, feel relaxed...

breathe out, feel calm...

Now bring the attention back to the body and start feeling your arms and legs once again. You can close your hands or move your fingers, just to take control of the space around you.

Please, keep the eyes closed for now and enjoy the beautiful moment you are living. You have given yourself the time to feel better and that is absolutely incredible.

Breathe in, feel relaxed...

breathe out, feel calm...

Breathe in, feel relaxed...

breathe out, feel calm...

Breathe in, feel relaxed...

breathe out, feel calm...

Breathe in, feel relaxed...

breathe out, feel calm...

Now become aware of the environment around you once again. Feel the different sounds, the temperature of the room you are in and once you are ready, open the eyes again.

Chapter 28 Peaceful, Calming and Relaxing Music for Relief, Anxiety and Stress

Welcome to this guided meditation, it has been designed to help you feel happy and confident inside. To help you let go of any inner fears or doubts.

Everyone feels sad or worried at times.

Sometimes life is good and at other times, life is more difficult. At times, you may doubt your abilities. You may compare yourself to others.

You may worry that you are not as clever .... or, as kind.

Perhaps you feel you are not as popular.

This can make you feel less confident.

Practice this meditation daily and your confidence will soar.

You will feel relaxed. Carefree and so contented.

Find a comfortable position in which to relax.

You can lie down or sit up if you prefer.

Make sure you have time to complete this meditation.

Just close your eyes and try to follow the sound of my voice.

Your mind may wander sometimes, don't worry, just try to pay attention again. Tuning into my voice as you continue this journey of pure discovery.

Breathe through your nose and feel your chest rising.

Breathe out through your mouth and feel your chest lower.

Try to feel a connection between the mind and the body.

Every muscle starts to relax.

You feel your muscles becoming heavier.

As if you are sinking...

Floating.

It is like daydreaming but not quite asleep.

Breathe in again, feeling the sensation as your lungs expand.

Now breathe out through your mouth and let your body relax and muscles go all limp.

You feel happy and this moment.

Very relaxed.

Calm and peaceful

You are going to transport yourself to the beach.

It is a wonderful hot day.

Not too hot but enough for people to go swimming.

Or to relax on the sand.

As you stand on the sand, you can see so many people lying in the sun.

Family groups. Young children creating sandcastles. Parents helping them shape sand into shapes.

You are so interested in what they are doing.

Gaining ideas for your own castles.

As you continue to look, there are people swimming and others playing in the water at the edge.

The water is a deep blue with frothy white tips as it hits the shore.

It ebbs and flows at a wonderful pace. In and out. It flows naturally and you feel drawn to play in the water, to splash about.

Feel the warmth from the sun on your skin.

The sun is a golden yellow ball in a beautiful clear blue sky.

There are no clouds to mar the view.

Everyone is so happy here.

You hear laughter and the sounds of the water breaking on the shore.

You are happy to be here.

You feel warm.

As you look down, you see that your bare feet are covered in sand.

It feels wonderful to have the warmth through your feet.

The sand between your toes.

Walk to the water and now feel the cool water over your feet, washing the sand away.

Even though there are so many people here, you feel that it is so peaceful.

There is happiness.

Laughter.

Seagulls fly noisily overhead.

White bodies against a blue sky. Large wings stretched out.

Soaring, dipping in and out of the waves.

Boats pass by, white sails a contrast against the blue horizon.

Someone is on jet skis.

There is so much happening. So much fun.

Take a moment to enjoy this beach scene.

Music to fade 40 seconds.

As you walk along the beach, you see amazing sand sculptures.

Wonderful works of art.

They exist in this wide expanse of sand.

Huge sandcastles take center place.

As if on show.

They have turrets and towers.

One has a moat around it.

And a drawbridge.

So much detail.

You can see how much work has gone into it.

You are creative, and you want to build the same, but you don't know how to do it.

As you look at other sand creations, you see, people have shaped faces and animals. There is so much detail. All made from sand.

You have never seen anything like this before. You long to be shown how to do it.

The desire to build a big sandcastle fills your mind.

Yours will be better than ever.

If you feel doubts about your abilities, let them go.

Just enjoy the pleasure of creating an image from sand.

Of sculpting.

Of being a sand artist.

You are so in the moment.

Happiness washes over you.

There is so much pleasure.

You fill a bucket with water and add sand to it.

Scooping the first handful to create a base on the sand. You can feel the wet sand on your fingers.

It feels rough.

Course against your skin.

You add more wet sand but, you cannot shape it…the block falls apart.

As you look around, you see what others are doing. Filling a hole in the sand with water. Sending sand into the center. They drain the sand.

You are learning.

Through watching others.

You take these lessons on board.

Take a moment here to think of your design.

Music to fade 30 seconds

Feel the warm sand in your fingers as you scoop out a hole. Fill the hole with water. Now, with your fingers, feel the sensation of wet, gritty sand against your hands. Now, make your shapes. Using the bucket to create solid turrets.

You keep building.

Enjoying the pleasure of creativity.

You are an artist. ^

Not with paints but with sand.

You love being here.

Learning

Happy in this moment.

Confidence growing as your sandcastle takes shape.

Even when some sand does not stay in shape, you learn from the experience.

You realize what you must do.

You are driven to complete the castle.

It continues to grow. Shape upon shape.

Growing taller.

Reaching up out from the sand.

You draw shapes of windows with a twig.

Patterns in the wall.

And a moat.

Now, you fill the moat with water…

You know it will drain but, for a moment, you feel your castle is real.

Something you have created.

For all to see.

You are an artist.

This is so relaxed.

So peaceful....

Even now as people start to leave.

You feel happy in this moment.

You achieved more than you thought you could.

By learning, by listening, by thinking.

Know that you are capable of anything.

You believe in yourself.

You know you can do whatever you want.

You are not afraid to try.

Trying is part of the experience.

Each experience is important to you.

Breathe in warm air and breathe out...fully...

You feel relaxed and so peaceful.

You feel happy in this moment.

As you stand back to view your castle, you know it is time to leave. But you feel wonderful. The sun is setting.... you watch it sinking towards the sea. The sky is now red streaked. It looks beautiful.

The sea is calm.

Gentle.

Boats are sailing back to the port.

It is time for you to go home. But always remember, you can come back here at any time you like. You just need to close your eyes.

Breathe in slowly and breathe out fully.

When ready, you can open your eyes.

Chapter 29 Short Stories Against Anxiety and Stress Helping the Adult Fall Asleep

Denmark is high up north, where Germany stops. There is still a king there today, but he is no longer there to govern, but usually visits kindergartens because his wife likes children so much.

But a long time ago, the Danish king was very powerful. As all kings used to do, he always wanted to increase his land so that he would become even more powerful. So, he also had to conquer another country. That was not easy. In the south of Denmark was Germany, then the kingdoms of Hanover and Prussia. He could not mess with them because they had many more soldiers than he. Likewise, the Swedes, whose country lies next to Denmark.

So, he looked north. Far behind the sea was Greenland. This is a huge country, but at the time it was very little known, and it was supposed to be very cold there. So, he had three ships loaded from the royal fleet. On each he put a brave knight and several soldiers, as well as horses and all kinds of war equipment.

Then it went off to Greenland in the terribly cold north. When the ships arrived, they first saw a lot of ice and snow. The knights put on their armor and went ashore to conquer it. But no one was visible, and the knights froze in their iron armor on the ice, so they could not move.

They kicked wildly, clawing their iron armor hard to free themselves from the ice.

A few of the other soldiers had to make a fire to get them released. As a result, of course, the armor on the feet were pretty hot and the knights burned their feet. They shopped around wildly until they were finally free and quickly disappeared on the ship.

Then one tried to bring the horses ashore, because one should conquer Greenland. The horses struggled hard, but after a few meters they also got stuck in the snow. The soldiers could not walk in the high snow and froze miserably, so that finally all went with their horses back on the ships and Greenland could not conquer first. When the knights sat around thinking and pondering, the lookout on the ship's mast reported "Enemy ahead !!"

And indeed, the knights saw in astonishment how a sleigh came with very small horses. They were astonished even more when they discovered that it was not horses but many dogs in front of a sled so effortlessly whizzing across the snow.

Everyone brought their rifles and lances and feared that they would have to defend themselves. But there was only one man on the sled, an Eskimo. He greeted them in a very friendly way and was happy to see so many people, because in Greenland not so many people live, and one is often quite lonely and alone. He welcomed everyone and asked them if they would not visit him in the evening, his wife would cook a nice soup of seal meat for them.

From whom you are greeted so friendly, you can fight badly against, and so put three of the knights on the dogsled, but without their heavy armor. Husch - you rushed over the landscape to a strange hut, which was made entirely of snow. It's called an igloo and it's round, but it's very nice and warm!

When they had eaten, they thanked each other, and the Eskimo drove them back to their ships by dog sled. Then it was decided to drive back to Denmark.

They then reported everything to the king. He held advice with his ministers how to conquer Greenland. They also asked a wise old man named Count Johannsen. The count whispered his suggestion in the ear of the king, and he was thrilled!

He sent his steward to the city to buy whatever vanilla powder he could get. Then he equipped a ship again, but this time the knights should put on thick fur coats and take sledges with them. In addition, the whole load compartment was full of vanilla powder!

Arrived in Greenland, they were greeted by Eskimos again, it was already known by now. The soldiers from Denmark brought a lot of fresh snow and made it with their vanilla powder from delicious vanilla ice cream. They gave it to the Eskimos.

They had never eaten anything like that! They were crazy about it and still wanted to have more. The knights, however, kept everything under wraps and first wanted to speak to the eskimo leader, who was quickly brought for them. With him, the knights made a contract that now

Greenland would belong to Denmark and for that the Eskimos would get as much vanilla ice cream as they could eat.

Then the knights sailed home with their ship and told their king that Greenland would now belong to Denmark, without there being a war!

And that's how it is today, so you can ask every Dane.

Chapter 30 Short Stories to Help Adult on Meditation, Relaxation and Fall Asleep Quickly

Visiting Paris in the spring is the ultimate in luxurious travel, and I plan to submerge myself entirely in the authentic Parisian experience. This is why I recruited a friend who recently relocated to the city of lights to host me for a few days and give me a tour of the favorite places they had discovered.

The plan is to meet at a cafe near my hotel, and I decide to dress my best. Comfort and style are needed to blend in with Parisians, so I wore my most fashionable ensemble. I know we will be walking all day, so I finish my outfit off with stylish, white sneakers. For good measure, from the souvenir shop in my hotel, I purchase a delicate silk scarf with a dash of orange and pale blue in the sizeable geometric pattern. I loosely tie it around my neck the way I've seen movie stars do and feel like I fit the role entirely.

My enthusiasm for the day is like a child on Christmas morning. I am ready ahead of time, so I walk to the cafe early and begin my Parisian experience. As I walk, the city comes alive through its residents going about their weekday routines. My hotel is on a corner. When I exit the lobby, the narrow street is populated with a few cars, and some cyclists squeezed into the even more narrow spaces for the bike lane. There is limited space to travel, but the morning commuters are peaceful and do not seem to be in a rush to get anywhere.

I walk through the neighborhood and see shopkeepers open their doors and windows to let in fresh air. The sky is a lovely bright blue speckled with the lightest dusting of wispy white clouds. It's a picture-perfect spring day. I cross a street and see the cafe already filling with patrons. A few people are outside reading the newspaper. Someone is sitting with their eyes closed, and their face toward the sun soaking in what I can guess is the first beautiful day this season. A woman is having a conversation with a person who has a small, fluffy, tan-colored dog who is not interested in chit-chat. The dog gently tugs on the leash to encourage their owner to move on to the exciting thing around the next corner.

Inside, the cafe is bright and welcoming, with plants spilling over the edges of their pots and colorful chairs tucked into wooden tables. In my best French I order a cappuccino, a croissant with jam and a glass of orange juice. The woman who takes my order repeats it to me in English, and we share a knowing glance of appreciation. She tells me to find a seat, and she will take my breakfast for me. On the patio, the woman talking to the dog walker has left, so I seat myself in her place. A few moments later, my server deliveries my first Parisian breakfast, I say merci and pause for a moment to take in the enjoyment of this moment.

The croissant is warm with a crisp golden exterior. When I pull it apart, I can see the steam release, telling me this pastry was freshly baked just moments ago. I savor each buttery bite in between sips of my creamy, dark, perfectly smooth cappuccino. With half of the decadent pastry gone, I spread a generous amount of the fresh strawberry jam onto my next bite. The tartness of the jam with the richness of the croissant is possibly the most delightful breakfast I've had in a long time. I feel very much like the natural Parisian of my dreams.

As I sip on the last of my freshly squeezed orange juice, my friend arrives. I rise to give them a long hug, we express how long it's been, and they complement me on my silk scarf. We tidy up my table, and I bring the empty dishes inside and wave goodbye to my lovely server. My friend links their arm in mine, and together, we walk through the streets of Paris, catching up on each other's lives since the last time we saw each other a few years back.

We pass through the Palace De La Bastille with its tall pillar celebrating the three-day revolution that saw the fall of one king and the rise of another. The tall post is topped with a golden statue of a man, perched delicately on one foot, and a hand raised into the sky in victory. The sun gleams across the flame is his raised hand and floods the plaza with its warmth.

After a short stroll, we come to the main attraction of our walk, the Le Viaduc des Arts, a collection of artisan shops built into the remnants of the old Paris-Bastille railways.

The brick structure is tall and stretches as far as I can see in a series of wide arches closed in with floor to ceiling windows and filled with unique creations in each different arch. The top of the bridge-like structure is a raised park filled with trees, water features, and an almost secret pathway that covers the entire length of the bridge. I can smell the roses blooming atop the building and struggle to decide which splendid sight to take in first. My friend and guide suggest we browse the workshops for half of the walk and enjoy the park for the rest of the journey.

Each archway holds a different treasure, from art restoration to custom made jewelry, perfumers, and jam makers to artists and craftspeople of all genres happily go about creating their work. Many are focused on their craft.

Those who are not busy smile as we press our faces close to the windows for a better look at the delicate nature of their work. Filled with awe and inspiration, we make our way up the stairs to the raised park and continue our walk surrounded by the early spring blooms of this secret garden.

We walk silently, content in the moment, and with each other's presence.

Near the end of the park, my friend asked if I was ready to see more of Paris. There is the Pantheon a few blocks up, the stunning Jardin du Luxembourg and all its statues, and of course, the Eiffel tower was not that far away. I gently rub the silk scarf I purchased that morning as I think and reply, "while in Paris my love," and we turn to make our way toward the exciting place around the next corner.

Conclusion

J ust like using medication, you will want to do these meditations consistently in order to get the best benefits possible. It took a while to create your pain. It doesn't always happen so quickly, so just as it took some time to create the mentality you have, it will take some time to reverse it.

If you stay dedicated to the healing process and focused on finding peace within yourself, you will discover an incredible ability to actually heal yourself. Don't wait around and simply hope that things will eventually get better. Take power back over your mind and let yourself become fully healed in this process.

We offer a plethora of other meditations that you can do for specific reasons. Whether you want to get a better night's sleep or are interested in losing weight through the healing process, you can find a meditation directed specifically at your needs. The only way that you will be able to enjoy a fulfilled and happy life is to let yourself be free from the things that cause so much anguish and pain.

Meditation has been a way of life in many cultures for centuries. It has helped millions of people in conducting their life in a meaningful way. It is a peaceful way of life that focuses on being mindful and aware.

Modern life has become so fast-paced that people have stopped rationalizing over the need for the actions they take. Everyone is following someone or the other. However, one solution fits all don't work when it comes to human beings. This has led to numerous problems. The biggest problem is that people are finding it increasingly difficult to focus and find a purpose in life. Meditation doesn't dictate a path to you. It is a way to develop the abilities to find the right path. It is an important tool using which you can become more successful in life.

Meditation has always been liked by monks who had no love for the material world. However, it is not the way of leaving everything out. It is the way in which you can get the most even while you don't have much. It teaches the most difficult art of being content.

We will prove to be your primer for meditation. It will tell you everything about meditation. From the right way to begin meditation to the various ways in which you can practice meditation as a beginner.

Meditation should not distance you from people, especially from your loved ones. Although many people these days meditate to relieve stress and feel better, the true effects of meditation are not really just for yourself, but also for others. Meditation should lead you to be kinder, express more love, and exercise compassion at all times. You must do so sincerely. The fact remains that even among those who meditate for years, only a few reach enlightenments in one lifetime. Therefore, although enlightenment may be your goal on why you meditate, never allow yourself to be obsessed with the idea of enlightenment. If you want to have less stress and live a happier life, then make peace with the people around you and show your love, even to your enemies.

Meditation will give you the strength that you need to do so. All forms of meditation also develop the heart chakra, which will allow you to be more compassionate and exercise universal love. Daily meditation practice can make you healthier, happier, and more successful than ever. Only a few minutes of meditation practice daily can help you lower stress, improve your mental and physical health, boost your focus and increase work productivity. If you heard about meditation but don't know how to begin – or you have practiced meditation in the past, but need help to get started again, this beginner's meditation guidebook is for you.

You may find benefit in learning to be a better-rounded individual with emotional intelligence, hoping to defeat your anxiety through learning social skills that can benefit you. You may find benefit in becoming more skilled at the techniques brought to your attention within this book. You may even prefer a book dedicated solely to cognitive behavioral therapy that can teach you the steps necessary to complete cognitive restructuring in detail.

You deserve to live a life that is one you can enjoy, free from worrying about what your friends think of you. Through spending the time and effort necessary, you can achieve that life that, up until this point, may have seemed like impossibility. It will not be easy, but it is possible for you. If you want it, all you have to do is reach for it and practice the steps provided within this book for you. With the effort necessary, you will begin to find relief from the symptoms, and if you do not, you are not out of options—a therapist or licensed medical professional can help you further. Just remember, there is always hope of getting out of this situation. All you have to do is ask for the help that is out there.

Meditation will help you become more disciplined and focused in everything you do. It will help you relax and take a break from all your troubles. It will help you to improve your physical, mental, and spiritual health over time.

The best part is that you will only have to give 10-15 minutes of your day just to reap all these rewards. So, find a quiet place and take the time to practice meditation from today forward. You will notice positive changes if you start sooner rather than later.

Printed in Poland
by Amazon Fulfillment
Poland Sp. z o.o., Wrocław